W9-BGL-968

...and turn it again

...and turn it again

Theme and Sacred Variations

Simeon J. Maslin

Copyright © 2008 by Simeon J. Maslin.

Library of Congress Control Number: 2008901737
ISBN: Hardcover   978-1-4363-0779-6
               Softcover   978-1-4363-0778-9

All rights reserved. No part of this book may be reproduced or transmitted in any form
or by any means, electronic or mechanical, including photocopying, recording, or by
any information storage and retrieval system, without permission in writing from the
copyright owner.

Biblical quotations, with minor exceptions, are taken from *Tanakh: A New Translation
of Holy Scriptures,* Jewish Publication Society, Philadelphia, 1985

This book was printed in the United States of America.

To order additional copies of this book, contact:
Xlibris Corporation
1-888-795-4274
www.Xlibris.com
Orders@Xlibris.com

44548

To Judith

Proverbs 31:28-29

Contents

Prescript

The title of this book, *. . . **and turn it again***, is taken from a well-known aphorism by a first-century Palestinian sage known as Ben Bag Bag,* found toward the end of the fifth chapter of *Pirke Avot* (*Sayings of the Fathers*). Speaking about the study of Torah, Ben Bag Bag said,

> *"Hafoch ba va-hafoch ba, d'chola ba—*
> Turn it and turn it again, for everything is in it.
> Contemplate it, grow old over it, and never depart from it,
> for there is no finer pursuit."

---

* Some scholars identify Ben Bag Bag with a certain Yochanan ben Bag Bag who is mentioned briefly in early rabbinic sources. It is possible that the Hebrew letters *bet-gimel* indicate that he was a *ben ger*, the son of a proselyte to Judaism. Some also identify him with the proselyte who asked the great sage Hillel to teach him the Torah "while standing on one foot." After hearing Hillel's summary of the Torah, "What is hateful to you, do not do to another," he followed Hillel's admonition to "Go and study."

Foreword

Theme and Sacred Variations

This is a book about Torah—not about *the* Torah, but about Torah. There is a difference.

Strictly speaking, the Torah is the Pentateuch, the Five Books of Moses, often referred to in Hebrew as *Humash*. The word Torah means "teaching or direction," and it is as old as the Torah itself. In the book of Deuteronomy alone, it appears fifteen times, in most cases referring to particular sets of laws but in a few cases referring to a collection of teachings that Moses had set before the people of Israel: *"This is the Torah that Moses set before the Israelites. These are the decrees, laws and rules that Moses addressed to the people of Israel, after they had left Egypt"* (Deut. 4:44).

Toward the end of Deuteronomy, there is a clear reference to a *sefer* (a book or a lengthy document) that Moses wrote before his death: *"Moses wrote down this Torah and gave it to the priests, sons of Levi, who carried the ark of Adonai's**

---

* I have attempted to avoid the masculine word Lord as a translation for the Hebrew Adonai in biblical verses. When Adonai is used in the text, it usually indicates a personal name of God, unlike the more general *Elohim* (or *El* or

x

covenant, and to all the elders of Israel" (Deut. 31:9). Without commenting here on the historicity or the unity of the Torah, topics that are addressed elsewhere in this book, when we say *the* Torah, we are referring to the five books, portions of which are read seriatim in synagogues each week.

There are, however, larger definitions for the word *Torah.* Although the traditional word, actually an acronym, for the entire Bible is *Tanakh* (Torah), *Neviim* (Prophets), and *Ketuvim* (Writings), it too is often referred to as Torah. When the sages of the Talmud needed a proof text to buttress an argument, they were as likely to select verses from the Prophets or the Writings (also known as the Hagiographa) as from *the* Torah. All were sacred scriptures; all were Torah.

There is yet a larger meaning to the word *Torah.* The sages of the Talmud felt certain that their interpretations of the Torah, what they had learned from their teachers as sacred traditions going back to Moses and the prophets, were also Torah. They called their deliberations and decisions Oral Torah, and as time went on, the Oral Torah (*Torah she-b'al peh*) took on almost the same degree of sanctity as the Written Torah (*Torah she-bikh'tav*).

And there is yet a larger definition for this rather elastic word. Back in 1943, Judith Eisenstein, daughter of the noted theologian Mordecai M. Kaplan, wrote an instructional cantata that she entitled *What Is Torah?* in which she cited a variety of cultural creations and distinguished Jews as "Torah." The cantata was very popular in the '40s and '50s, often performed at religious school assemblies and graduations. A generation later, we often joked about one of the lines in that cantata: "*What is Torah? Menahem Mendel Ussishkin.*" I enjoyed referring to it facetiously as the greatest line in English literature. Today, there is not one Jew in a hundred who can tell you that Mr. Ussishkin was a well-known early Zionist, a widely read pamphleteer, and the president of the Jewish National Fund. But even conceding his erstwhile prominence, what was Eisenstein suggesting when she included Ussishkin in her definition of Torah? Clearly, she believed that all serious Jewish culture—religion, literature, ethics, and even politics, all that added to the vibrancy of Judaism and that might be a response to God—was Torah.

Eloah) which I translate as God. And so whenever the name Adonai or the Tetragrammaton (the unspoken four-letter name YHVH) appears in a text, I do not translate it but simply reproduce Adonai.

And so we see that Torah means far more than the Five Books of Moses or even the Bible with all its commentaries. Every generation of Jews is capable of adding to the definition of Torah, as long as the starting point of the creative process is the Torah itself. Torah is the leitmotif, the unifying theme of Judaism, and all of the writings of the sages and prophets and poets and teachers of Judaism are variations on that venerable theme. And here we come to the title that I chose for this volume, . . . *and turn it again.*

There are 24 books* and 23,232 verses in the Bible. Scholars and laypeople have been studying them, parsing them, arguing about them, taking inspiration from them, and regarding them with awe for well over two thousand years. Ben Bag Bag (see Prescript) was one of those scholars, certainly not the greatest but one who found new meaning in those beloved verses every time that he read and reread them. Picture a scholar holding the *atzei hayim*, the rollers to which the sacred text is attached, bending over the parchment as he turns to the next column, and suddenly realizing that this or that verse could mean something other than what he was taught. What a thrill! And not only is the scholar delighted with his new insight, but I believe, God too is delighted. With each turning, with each variation, with each new and deeper revelation, we come closer to the mind of God.

The process of reading a verse or a story from Torah and then expanding it with some new insight or some commentary that goes beyond its face value is called midrash. The sages called the simple meaning of a text *peshat* and the newer or deeper meaning *derash* or midrash. Here are two brief examples of midrashic variations:

---

*   Talmudic tradition has it that there are twenty-four books in the Bible. Some, though, may count thirty-nine. In either count, we are referring to the same books. In the larger count, the Twelve Minor Prophets are counted individually, as are the books of 1 and 2 Samuel, 1 and 2 Kings, and 1 and 2 Chronicles. The twenty-four, as enumerated in the Talmud (*Baba Batra* 14b), are the five books of the Torah (Genesis, Exodus, Leviticus, Numbers and Deuteronomy), the eight books of the Prophets (Joshua, Judges, Samuel, Kings, Isaiah, Jeremiah, Ezekiel and the Twelve), and the eleven books of the Writings (Psalms, Proverbs, Ruth, Ecclesiastes, Song of Songs, Lamentations, Esther, Job, Daniel, Ezra-Nehemiah, and Chronicles).

1. The story of Korah, the man who (Num. 16) led a rebellion against Moses in the desert, begins with these two Hebrew words *Va-yikah Korah*, which means "and Korah took." The text continues to identify Korah and his cohort without offering any object for the verb "took." Took what? And so a variety of solutions are offered. Rashi, the great medieval commentator, suggested that Korah took himself to a different side, in opposition to Moses. One modern translation reads: "Now Korah . . . betook himself," and another has it: "And Korah took men . . ." The skeptic will suggest that some ancient scribe simply made a mistake and left out whatever it was that Korah took, but with that suggestion he forfeits a perfect opportunity for midrash, adding something that is missing from the text in order to elucidate it or even to spice it up a bit.

2. In the well-known story of Jacob's dream, in Genesis 28:12, the text reads, "A stairway was set on the ground, and its top reached to the sky, and angels of God were going up and down on it." You might not see any problem in this simple text (aside, of course, from some puzzlement about angels), but Rashi did. He asked, "Going up and then going down?" You see, if there are such heavenly creatures as angels, one would expect them to come down from heaven before they could go up again. And so, Rashi's solution: "The angels who watched over Jacob in the holy land were not allowed to go out of the land, and so they had to go back up to heaven [at the point when Jacob was about to leave for Mesopotamia]. They were then replaced with angels who were allowed to go outside of the land to continue watching over him."

These two examples of "turn it and turn it again," the midrashic process which enriches virtually every verse of Torah, lead me to an autobiographical note that might explain my own love for midrash. When I was a little boy, my father, the principal of our Hebrew school, employed a fine young college student, Abe Ruderman, to teach in the school and to conduct services for the children's congregation on Shabbat. Abe, who later became a Reform rabbi, was a wonderful storyteller and each Shabbat, he would captivate the kids with stories based on the Torah portion of the week. Abe, though, stayed at our house through Shabbat, and invariably in the afternoon while my parents were taking their Shabbat naps, he would accede to my requests for yet another story, one for me alone. And that's how I came to know about Eldad and Medad.

Who were Eldad and Medad? In Numbers, chapter 11, there is a story about these two men who, among seventy, received the gift of prophecy from God. The purpose of this gift was so that they might ease some of the burden of leadership from the shoulders of Moses. But Eldad and Medad could not resist showing off their new powers in the midst of the Israelite camp, to the consternation of Joshua who advised Moses to imprison them. But Moses, in effect, told Joshua to cool it, adding the memorable aspiration: *"If only all of Adonai's people could be prophets."* That is the entire story, four brief verses, and there is no further mention of these two exhibitionists in the Bible.

The fact, though, that we know nothing more about Eldad and Medad did not inhibit Abe. To him, they were mischievous boys who got into one scrape after another and somehow always cleverly managed to wriggle their way out of trouble. By the end of each weekly Eldad and Medad story, quite without realizing it, I had absorbed some new moral lesson and a few more words of Hebrew. It wasn't until a few decades later that I realized that Abe's pedagogic method was midrash, the embroidery of stories and morals onto the fabric of Torah. He took that brief text and turned it and turned it yet again, initiating one curious little boy into a process that continues in these pages.

I have been richly blessed throughout my life with teachers like Abe Ruderman, of blessed memory, my father, professors, and students who have encouraged me to continue to "turn it and turn it again," carrying on the sacred art of midrash. I read a biblical verse for possibly the hundredth time, and I am suddenly confronted by a new possibility. Rashi, the master commentator, wrote in several instances of verses that cried out to him, "*Darsheni* (Interpret me)!" (Gen. 25:22 and 37:20 are notable examples.) I know that feeling well. Often, as I am reading or teaching Torah, it is as if I can hear a voice calling out to me: "Stop, Shimon! There is more to me than meets the eye. Let's talk it over." And so we turn it over again—and again.

There are twenty-four books in the Hebrew Bible, and by way of homage to the sacred text, I have chosen to limit myself to twenty-four turnings of the *atzei hayim*. The verses that I have selected for this volume are taken from only about half of the twenty-four, and they are among the hundreds that have cried out to me at one time or another: *Darsheni!* (Interpret me). But we'll begin with these, keeping in mind the words of Hillel, Ben Bag Bag's teacher: *Puk, hazi* (now go and study).

Turn 1

This is My God, and I Will Glorify Him, the God of My Father, and I Will exalt Him.*

—Exodus 15:2

---

* We have made every effort to avoid gender references to God, but in some cases, the Hebrew original makes it virtually impossible to use any pronoun other than "Him."

Menahem Mendl of Kotsk, one of the outstanding leaders of early nineteenth-century Hassidism, was reared by a learned father who was an outspoken opponent of Hassidism. When he realized that his young son was veering away from normative Judaism toward Hassidism, he rebuked him and attempted to bring him back to the fold. But young Menahem Mendl responded to his father's admonitions by quoting a verse from Exodus 15 along with a novel commentary:

> *This is my God, and I will glorify Him,*
> *the God of my father, and I will exalt him.*

"*This is my God,*" he explained, "means that I must search for God in ways that have meaning for *me* personally, so that I can glorify God with integrity. Then and only then can I truly exalt "*the God of my father.*"

Clearly, the author of the triumphant "Song of the Sea" did not have the conflict between the generations in mind when he or she (possibly Miriam?) sang out so lustily to the God who had defeated the Egyptians. The magnificently bellicose verses of Exodus 15 found their way into the daily and Passover liturgies of Judaism, both in their entirety and in notable selections (e.g., *Mi Kamokha*), and they even provided the name for one of the greatest American thoroughbreds, Man o' War. The popular novelist, Herman Wouk, used *"This is My God"* for the name of his exposition of traditional Judaism and then followed up with a workbook entitled *And I Will Glorify Him.* But in none of this is there even a hint of the Kotsker's interpretation.

When I first came across that exchange between Rabbi Menahem Mendl and his father, it reminded me of an exchange between my learned Orthodox father and myself back in 1974. My father disapproved of any form of Judaism other than modern Orthodoxy, and so he was very disappointed and critical when I decided to enter the Reform rabbinate. He never allowed his criticism to become hurtful to me personally, but he made it quite clear that he did not consider Reform to be a legitimate expression of Judaism. And so he never attended a service that I conducted and he never heard me deliver a sermon.

My father retired to Jerusalem in 1970, and he was there when the Reform rabbinate met in Jerusalem for its convention in 1974. Of course, I looked forward to the opportunity of visiting with him, but I avoided telling him that I would be delivering a lecture at the convention. My assigned topic was the extent to which the modern state of Israel was, or was not, living up to prophetic ideals of social justice, and there was no way that I could avoid being critical of the way that the Orthodox political parties hobbled efforts by successive Israeli governments to address issues of human rights for the benefit of all. Somehow, though, my father discovered that I would be delivering a lecture and he informed me that since he had never been able to hear me preach in my synagogue, he was eagerly looking forward to hearing me lecture in a secular venue. I told him that it might be better for him not to be present at that particular lecture, but he was insistent.

I will confess that I did briefly consider softening my critique of Orthodoxy so as not to offend my father, but I decided that I could not in good conscience do so. As I delivered the lecture, I looked over at him a couple of times as he sat there attentive but expressionless. When I finished, I saw him rise and head for the door. (He had told me beforehand that he had a meeting of the tzedakah committee that he chaired later that afternoon at the offices of the chief rabbinate.) But as he was about to pass through the door, he turned to me, waved and, with thumb and forefinger, made a clear gesture of approval. I was truly baffled; I knew that there was no way that my father could have approved of a good part of my message, yet he had made that gesture.

That evening I called my father and I asked him what he meant by his gesture. Did he accept my critique of Israeli Orthodoxy? "No no," he answered. "I didn't agree at all with what you said, but I loved the way that you said it!" Through this and other incidents after my decision to leave Orthodoxy for Reform, I knew that while my father disapproved of my religious choice, he approved of my search for God according to my own lights.

*   *   *

Most people find it hard to believe that nowhere in the Bible is there a commandment to believe in God. The Bible does give examples of people who believed in God and who thus earned the love and approval of God. Abraham is a notable example: *"Because he [Abraham] put his trust in Adonai, He reckoned it to his merit"* (Gen. 15:6). But neither the belief in God nor any other belief is put forth in the Bible as a commandment. We are commanded to observe God's Sabbath, to refrain from lying, from adultery, from stealing and from murdering, to celebrate various festivals, to practice justice, and to share our bounty with the poor, etc., etc. There are hundreds of commandments (tradition puts the figure at 613) in the Bible covering everything from the proper way to dress to the treatment of birds, but we are never commanded to believe.

One can only conclude that the authors of scripture understood that belief cannot be legislated. Their argument, if indeed they felt the need to argue at all, was very much like that of the theologian who maintains that the proof for the existence of a clockmaker is the clock itself. *"When God began to create heaven and earth"*—if there is a heaven and an earth, then there must be a Creator of heaven and earth, QED.

The Torah itself discourages speculation about the nature of God. When Moses, seemingly frustrated by the awesome task of convincing a stubborn people to accept the mandates of a god whom they could not see, asked God for some tangible evidence of existence, God replied with frustrating ambivalence. Moses asked,

> *"Now if I have truly gained Your favor, pray let me know Your ways . . . Let me behold Your presence." And [God] answered, "I will make all My goodness pass before you, . . . But you cannot see My face for a human may not see Me and live . . . As My presence passes by, I will put you in a cleft of the rock and shield you with My hand until I have passed by. Then I will take My hand away, and you will see My back; but My face must not be seen."* (Exod. 33:13-23)

It is virtually impossible to overlook the anthropomorphism that pervades that passage. God has a hand and a face and a back and, of course, as in numerous other passages in the Bible, God speaks. But one must not be put off by that rather primitive divine anatomy lesson; the sages taught that "the Torah speaks in the language of human beings," and human beings in the age when the Torah stories were first told could not have comprehended a totally metaphysical god. And so what does that passage teach us today?

It teaches that we should not attempt to define or quantify God. If God is God, then God is beyond human definition; we "cannot see God's face." There is no systematic theology in the Bible or in the vast Talmudic literature. Theology was not a Jewish science until medieval times when Judaism was challenged by the rival faiths of Islam and Christianity, the former in particular. It was not until Rabbi Saadiah Gaon (tenth century Babylonia) wrote his *Emunot ve-Deot* (*Beliefs and Opinions*) that Judaism began to posit particular beliefs about the nature of God.

Saadiah and others who followed him attempted to, as it were, "describe God" in terms that would respond to Aristotelianism and the Islamic Kalam theology that was so very influential in the ninth century. But Judaism was always very uncomfortable with attempts to characterize God. This discomfort is most evident in the writings of Maimonides, who taught (*Guide for the Perplexed*) that one must never attempt to describe God in positive terms; one is permitted to say what God is not, but not what God is. "None but God can understand what God is" (*Guide* 1:59). Or as the fifteenth-century theologian, Joseph Albo, put it: "If I knew God, I would be God."

Now what does all of this have to do with the rebellion of the young Menahem Mendel two centuries ago or my own rebellion half a century ago? The fathers against who we rebelled intellectually were our teachers; they taught us to love God and to observe the mitzvot. But neither of them demanded that we believe some dogmatic formulation of the nature of God. They taught us to be good Jews and good human beings, but never did they teach us that the rejection of any particular item of faith would condemn us to damnation. And so we were able to construct for ourselves systems of Judaism which, though departures from their beliefs, yet retained the essence.

I feel certain that as the Kotsker grew older, he, as I, realized how much he loved his father and how much he owed to him. In my case, that love and reverence grew stronger, paradoxically, the more that I departed from the details of my father's teachings. Why? Because it was my father who set me out on the path of inquiry. It was he who gave me the basic tools and who encouraged my curiosity. That I ended up in a place far from the practices of my father saddened him, but it did not cause a rift between us because he knew that I too loved God. (I can hear my father responding to that idea by saying, "Yes, *zunele*, you love God in *your* way, and I love God in *God's* way!")

One more anecdote about the relationship between my father and myself. When I made the decision to study for the Reform rabbinate, I did not know how to tell my parents. And so I devised a rather cowardly stratagem: I waited until they were overseas on a vacation, and I sent a letter addressed to them at the port of Le Havre. I hoped that they, and particularly my father, after reading my intentions, would calm down during the five-day return voyage. I was then a graduate student at the University of Pennsylvania, and I took the train to New York to meet their ship when it docked. After our reunion, I informed my parents that I would be catching a plane in just five hours to Cincinnati for my initial interview at Hebrew Union College-Jewish Institute of Religion.

We took a taxi to my sister's apartment in Upper Manhattan, and my father immediately led me by the hand into her bedroom where he proceeded to importune me for the next three hours not to go to Cincinnati (or Sodom, as he called it). He laid out every possible argument for the efficacy and beauty of Orthodoxy and the sterility, as he put it, of Reform, but I had made up my mind. When the time came for me to leave, he accompanied me to the subway station, arguing every step of the way. He continued even as we walked down the steps together and continued to the turnstiles. Finally, he stopped trying to dissuade me and he asked me, his wallet in his hands: "Do you have enough money to get there?" And we embraced.

*   *   *

There is a well-known prayer in the Jewish siddur which is called *Avot*, the Patriarchs. (In recent liberal prayer books, the title has been expanded to *Avot ve-Imahot* (*the Patriarchs and Matriarchs*) and the names of Sarah, Rebekah, Rachel, and Leah accompany those of Abraham, Isaac, and Jacob.) The prayer that I am referring to is the opening paragraph of what is known as the *Tefillah* (the Prayer, indicating the central prayer of the liturgy). It is also referred to as the *Amidah*, the Standing Prayer, and has been the core prayer of each of the three daily services since about the first century.

The traditional *Tefillah* begins by invoking "the God of Abraham, the God of Isaac, and the God of Jacob (*Elohei Avraham, Elohei Yitzhak, v'Elohei Yaakov*)."

An obvious question: in a religion that puts great portent on every utterance of the name of God, why is that name repeated for each of the patriarchs separately (and for each of the four matriarchs in the liberal prayer books)? Why does it not say, "God of Abraham, Isaac, and Jacob?" Would that not mean the same thing and avoid the overuse of the name of God? But no, there is a very important lesson to be learned from the connection of the name of God to each of the patriarchs individually.

Abraham was the pioneer who discovered God and struggled at Sodom and at Mount Moriah to understand his new and mysterious God. His entire life was devoted to the quest for "the Judge of all the earth." Ultimately, he achieved a wonderful faith in God, a faith that he transmitted to his son, Isaac.

If Isaac had been content to worship the God taught to him by his father, he would not have been worthy for inclusion among the patriarchs of Israel. Through the struggles of his lifetime and the new wisdom that he acquired in his generation, he expanded on the concept of God. True, Isaac prayed to the same God as Abraham, but Isaac had a greater understanding of God than Abraham did. He added new dimensions of paternal love and ultimate self-sacrifice to the faith of his father. Similarly, Jacob received the knowledge of God from his father, Isaac. But Jacob expanded that knowledge with the wisdom that he acquired in servitude for the sake of love, with the moral strength that he acquired wrestling with divinity, and with the empathy that he acquired as the father of contentious children. And so Jacob's understanding of God added even greater depth to the faith of Israel than did father Isaac or grandfather Abraham.

God does not change, but the human understanding of God grows, or *should* grow, with the life experience and the expansion of knowledge of each successive generation. And so it is that Jewish tradition prescribes that we invoke the God of Abraham *and* the God of Isaac *and* the God of Jacob. Each generation begins with the faith bequeathed by the previous generation, but if the heir to the tradition merely accepts the wisdom of the past, he or she has not fulfilled the mitzvah of loving God with all one's heart, soul, and might. One must accept but then struggle with the faith of the past in order to be a coworker with God in the ongoing process of creation. Each time that we speak the ancient words of the *Avot*, we are, in effect, pledging that we will add our own life stories to the story of God.

This is my God—I have studied and struggled and have finally been blessed with a vision of God that inspires me to work for a better and nobler society.

The God of my father—That is where I began my studies and my struggle, with the God taught to me by my father. But that inherited faith, great as it was, was tainted with tribal particularism, with a reverence for ritual over social responsibility, and with an unwillingness to recognize the sacredness of so many human achievements in the centuries since antiquity. The solid foundation of faith bequeathed to me by my father is an incomparable blessing, but in gratitude for that blessing, it is my sacred responsibility to achieve a deeper faith, a faith that may truly glorify God for the human family of my generation.

Turn 2

I dwell among my own people.

—2 Kings 4:13

It may be because I grew up during the uncertain years of the Holocaust that this simple verse from 2 Kings is so meaningful to me. I have always experienced the communities in which I have lived with mixed feelings of serenity and unease. Could it be that my usual sense of "at homeness" in this country is naive? Is it possible that there might ever be in America the kind of upheaval that would eventually, or even suddenly, turn me into an outcast, a pariah? I allow those occasional apprehensions to drift to the back of my mind, calmed by daily assurances that I do indeed "dwell among my own people."

- The doorman greets me with his usual "good morning" and adds, "Hey, the Sox won their third straight last night!" I return his greeting and say, "Yeah, but the Yanks won too." His response: "But the Sox will take the Yanks in the play-offs, I think this is the year." I grunt and say, "Don't bet the farm" and proceed down the street.

- I drop into the deli and as soon as I am seated, the waitress comes over, wishes me good morning, and sets down a cup of coffee at my place. I respond to her greeting and continue, "Two over light with a bagel, dry." She nods and a few minutes later, I am enjoying my breakfast.

- I am in a strange city, having arrived a few hours early for my lecture. I spot a policeman standing at the corner just outside of my hotel, and I ask him for directions to the nearest bookstore. "Well," he says affably. "There's a Barnes and Noble about three blocks straight ahead, and for the Borders, cross the street, go down one block, and then two to the left. Take your pick." I thank him and I'm on my way.

- I deliver the fiftieth reunion memorial address from the pulpit of Harvard's Memorial Church, concluding with the Kaddish and the predominantly Christian congregation answers, "*Amen*."

"I dwell among my own people."

A few summers ago, I was bottom-fishing with my grandson Beni a couple of miles out from the Harpswell shore in Casco Bay. They weren't biting, so we reeled in and I started up the engine to find a better spot. When I pushed the gear lever forward, nothing happened. I went through the procedure a few more times and each time, nothing. It took me only a few minutes to exhaust what little knowledge I have of engines, and we could see no other boats within hailing distance. The seas were calm, but I knew that there was always the danger of a wind whipping up and driving us toward the ledges lurking off Bailey Island. If necessary, I could throw out the anchor, but I decided that it would be prudent to call the coast guard on my cell phone.

My call was answered by someone at a base in Norfolk, Virginia, and after I gave him my position (thank God for GPS!), he told me to stand by while he radioed the base in Portland to inform them of our situation. I was listening to his call and offering additional information when my grandson tapped me on the shoulder and pointed toward the southwest. There, less than a mile off and closing rapidly, was a coast guard cutter! I couldn't believe my eyes, and I told the two guardsmen on the phone that I didn't know how they did it, but there was a cutter headed toward us. The Portland voice said, "The crews at sea monitor our conversations. One of them must be in your vicinity and heard you giving me your position. How far off is he?" I answered, "About half a mile now," and he said, "Please stay on the line until they're alongside and then give me their number."

The cutter, with a crew of four, arrived within a few minutes, and the last words that I heard from the Portland station were "You're in good hands now, sir. Have a good day."

My grandson helped one of the guardsmen tie onto our boat, and then the officer in charge asked me: "Permission to come aboard, sir?" At that moment, I nearly burst into tears. No, not that I was worried about our safety; I had no such concern. The seas were calm, and there were a good five hours to sunset. It was something else, something that I could only think about once we were back home and I could mull over the entire episode at leisure. As for the officer, he did indeed come aboard with my consent, and after tinkering in the engine compartment for a few minutes, he informed me that the gear coupling had broken and that the repairs would have to be made at a marina. He apologized for the fact that he was not allowed to tow us in, but he volunteered to call one of the local towboat companies, and he told me that he and his crew would stand by until the towboat arrived to make sure that we were safe. It was only when we were secured to the towboat that the cutter pulled away, the crew having wished us a good day.

What triggered that welling up of emotion that had me almost in tears when the coast guard officer posed his routine "permission to come aboard"? My mind had somehow transported me for an instant to the narrow straits between Denmark and the Swedish ports of Malmo and Goteborg, September 1943. Night after night that month, Danish fishing boats with cargoes of frightened Jews sailed across those narrow waterways, carefully avoiding German patrol boats. I cannot imagine the captain of one of those German boats, after overtaking a fishing boat, requesting "permission to come aboard."

Jews lived in peace and security in Denmark for hundreds of years before those horrendous nights of flight across the Kattegat and the Sund. They too had dwelt among their own people, in a country distinguished for its adherence to the highest standards of social justice. Yet they became victims overnight. And yes, multitudes of Jews in Weimar Germany, Hungary, Czechoslovakia, and Italy also thought that they were dwelling among their own people. They were tragically wrong.

The early chapters of 2 Kings recount a series of miracles performed by Elisha after he inherited the mantle of prophecy from his mentor, Elijah. In chapter 4, we read about a woman from the town of Shunem who extended hospitality to Elisha whenever he passed nearby. After several visits, Elisha wanted to reward her generosity, and so he instructed his servant, Gehazi, to ask her what they could do for her. *"Can we speak on your behalf to the king or to the army commander?"* And she answered in four very simple Hebrew words: *"B'tokh ami anokhi yoshavet* (I dwell among my own people)." That's it. No further explanation was necessary. She needed nothing. Why? Because she dwelt among her own people.

What did it mean, in biblical times, to dwell among one's own people? By way of contrast, consider the story of Abraham. What was his initial test of faith? God directed him: *"Go forth from your land, from your birth place, and from your father's house to the land that I will show you"* (Gen. 12:1); Abraham had been living in comfort and security in Haran. That Abraham (actually Abram at that time) was a member of one of the noble families of Haran is clear from the fact that Haran was not only the name of the city but also of his brother. (There are several ancient examples of royalty and their cities sharing names, see, for example, the story of Dinah and the prince, Shekhem; ibid., 34:2). Clearly, Abraham was a man of substance in Haran (see 12:5).

Abraham's departure from Haran to an unknown land, far removed from his family base and from the power and culture of Mesopotamia, was an act of great courage. *"He put his trust in Adonai, and [Adonai] reckoned it to his merit"* (ibid., 15:6). This divine encomium came *before* the dramatic tests of Abraham's faith at the destruction of Sodom and at the sacrificial altar on Mount Moriah. To depart from one's community and tribe was virtually a sentence of death in antiquity. Consider the dire punishments of ostracism in ancient Athens and exile in ancient Rome. Joseph's brothers intended at first to kill him, but they later decided that selling him to traders who would take him to a foreign land would solve their problem with him; he would be as good as dead (ibid., 37:27). And what was it that so impressed Boaz about Ruth of Moab? *"You left your father and mother and the land of your birth and came to a people you had not known before. May Adonai reward your deeds"* (Ruth 2:11f).

Back now to the woman of Shunem. The people of Elisha's day were surely aware of the dangers involved in leaving one's family and native land and conversely, the security of living in your birth community. And so we understand what the hospitable Shunemite meant when she replied to Elisha's offer of intercession with the authorities by responding simply and tersely, *"I dwell among my own people."* In other words, I need nothing. I have no use for the protection of the king or the commander of the army because I am a member of a family, a community, a tribe that accepts me, that understands me, and that will always defend me and provide for my social security. She had the faith and the serenity of the psalmist who sang, *"Adonai is my shepherd, I lack nothing."* Such is the enviable confidence of knowing that one does, indeed, dwell among one's own people.

But was she right to be so confident, even dwelling among her own people? Continuing her story, we find her just a few verses later in deep distress. Elisha had rewarded her kindness with the miraculous (she was beyond the age of childbirth) birth of a son. But after a few years, the boy had what seems like a sudden stroke and died. After a life of confident serenity, she needed help. *"As the Lord lives and as you live, I will not leave you,"* she insisted, clutching the feet of the prophet. Elisha understood that another miracle was required and so he hurried to her home and performed what seems like mouth-to-mouth resuscitation on the boy and revived him. And so we see that even a person who is confident that he/she lacks nothing and who enjoys the security of family and community can suddenly be struck by catastrophe and require assistance.

Out of the millions of Holocaust victims, there were surely tens of thousands who could have emigrated from Western Europe in the thirties but who chose to remain because they were confident that they dwelt among their own people. They were wrong. No one could have foretold the utter devastation in the wake of the 2004 tsunami in the Indian Ocean. Families who had lived confidently in their seaside villages for generations were suddenly decimated. Our lives hang by a thread even in the best of times, and as much as I admire and even covet the serene confidence of the Shunemite woman, was there possibly a measure of hubris in her response to Elisha's offer of protection? Don't we all need more than the goodwill of family and community? What about faith in God? The Shunemite woman said nothing about reliance on God. Was it possibly that omission that brought her so close to tragedy?

I banter about sports with a doorman, I experience an unspoken rapport with a waitress, I approach a policeman with confidence, I draw a mixed congregation into my particular ritual—this is my county! I am at home. I am! And yet . . . and yet my tears are triggered when a coast guard officer makes a routine request. The dark clouds of the early forties linger. They refuse to dissipate. Will I ever have the chutzpah to declare with the Shunemite woman, *I dwell among my own people?* And if I do so, will I perhaps have reason to regret misplaced confidence? Perhaps . . .

Turn 3

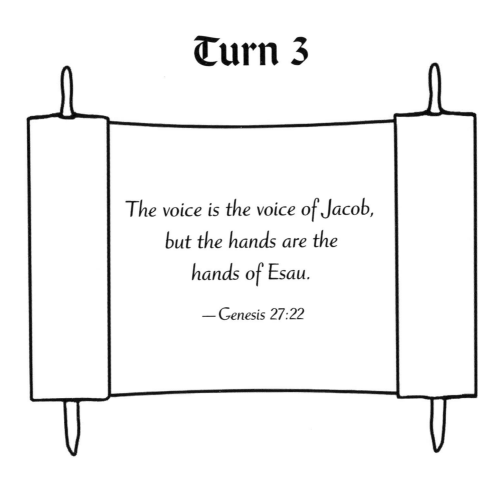

The voice is the voice of Jacob, but the hands are the hands of Esau.

—Genesis 27:22

One might read the story of Isaac and conclude that he is really not worthy of inclusion along with Abraham and Jacob among the patriarchs of the Jewish people. The book of Genesis devotes fourteen chapters to the saga of Abraham and ten full chapters and parts of several others to Jacob. But although he is often mentioned in the Torah along with his father and his son, there is only one chapter, Genesis 26, that is devoted almost entirely to the story of Isaac. The meager material on Isaac in the Torah seems to serve as little more than a bridge between the rugged iconoclasm of Abraham and the heroic struggles of Jacob/Israel.

Isaac seems always to be acted *upon* rather than acting. His very name, *Yitzhak*, is derived from *tzhok* (laughter). Mother Sarah, as you will recall, laughed when told that she, at her advanced age, would bear a child. And then when Isaac was a little boy, his mother drove the concubine, Hagar, and Isaac's half-brother, Ishmael, out of their camp because she feared that Ishmael might lead her precious little Isaac astray. And of course, one of the most basic and compelling stories in the patriarchal saga is the one known as the *Akeda* (the Binding) in which Isaac is the intended victim, splayed on the sacrificial altar. Not only was Isaac passive through that ordeal, he was more than slightly naive. He accepted his father's assurance that some animal would suddenly appear to be offered on the altar.

A few chapters later in Genesis, the time comes for Isaac to get married. Actually, the time was rather late; the text informs us that Isaac was already forty when Abraham realized that he was not capable of finding a wife for himself. You will recall that Abraham sent a trusted servant to Mesopotamia to find a proper wife for Isaac. And what did Isaac do when the servant returned with Rebekah? He installed her into the tent of his deceased mother, Sarah, and as the text puts it, *"He thus found comfort after his mother's death."*

There is even the implication in the text that Isaac, unlike his father, Abraham, and his son, Jacob, was not virile. Just before the Isaac story, we are told that Abraham, after the death of Sarah, sired six more sons with his new wife, Keturah. And of course, we all know about the twelve sons and at least one daughter of Jacob. (Abraham and Jacob may have had more daughters, but the Torah usually omits the names of daughters unless they, like Dinah, play some role in the story.) With Isaac, by contrast, we read of only one siring and that one only after years of effort and prayer. Finally, Rebekah bore him twins, Jacob and Esau, and the story shifts immediately away from Isaac to his sons.

Even that one chapter of Genesis that is devoted to the Issac story repeats a twice-told story from the saga of Abraham. And in that one chapter, God appears to Isaac and says very tenderly, *"I am the God of your father, Abraham; fear not, for I am with you."* Is it any wonder that several modern literary critics have suggested that Isaac is the classic prototype of the schlemiel, the antihero? Saul Bellow and Kafka and others have created protagonists who are anything but heroic. They are victims, harmless, passive people to whom things happen. In a lighter vein, the Isaac figure appears over and over again in the biting comedy of Woody Allen, once, in fact, (in the movie *Manhattan*) by the name of Ike or Isaac.

And so how did it happen that Jewish tradition for these thousands of years has linked the passive Isaac to the powerfully active Abraham and Jacob?

Is it possible that the story of the meek and gentle Isaac might be at least as relevant and instructive for us today as the stories of the fearless pioneer, Abraham, and the virile God-wrestler, Jacob? I believe so. It was the task of Isaac to keep alive the dynamic heritage of his father and to transmit it to one of his two problem sons. That he somehow succeeded in this task is attested to by the fact that Jews to this very day pray to *Elohei Avraham, Elohei Yitzhak, v'Elohei Yaakov*—the God of Abraham, the God of Isaac, and the God of Jacob. So how did he do it?

In that one chapter that deals with Isaac, there is a seemingly bland verse that reveals a lot about his strength of character. It reads, *"Isaac returned and dug again the wells which had been dug in the days of his father, Abraham, and which the Philistines had stopped up after Abraham's death."* What was it about the Philistines of antiquity that has caused people since their day to invoke their name when describing assaults on civilization? We refer to people who oppose the support of cultural institutions, who revel in ignorance and deride the pursuit of knowledge, as Philistines. In the Bible, the Philistines were those coastal people who harassed the Israelites from the days of the patriarchs through the periods of the judges and kings until the destruction of Jerusalem by the Babylonians. And so what does the Genesis text mean when it tells us that Isaac dug again the wells of Abraham that had been stopped up by the Philistines?

A homiletic interpretation: Abraham spent his life, as it were, digging wells, making available to his people and to those who passed through their territory the water which is essential for life. Abraham found the land to which God directed him a spiritual desert, and he left it well watered. But then Abraham died and the land was in danger of relapsing into barbarity. There were Philistines in the land, and they stopped up those wells of Abraham. Isaac did not have the pioneering strength of his father; he was not capable of digging new wells. But he understood that it was his sacred obligation at least to repair the wells of his father. And so Isaac searched out those wells that had been dug by his dynamic father, those wells of life-sustaining water that had been stopped up by the Philistines, and he hewed them out again.

There are times when no retreat is the greatest possible advance. This may be just such a time in history. Where are the Abrahams and Isaiahs today? Where are the Michelangelos and the Bachs, the Jeffersons and the Lincolns, the Freuds and the Einsteins, the Gandhis and Roosevelts and Ben-Gurions? We seem to be living in a generation of little people, of moral midgets whose overriding concern is personal success. Politics, business, and industry are dominated by people contemptuous of the general welfare, slaves of the bottom line, with attitudes of ethics be damned. Even the religious world is infested with evangelists who sell healing for a price, priests who abuse the innocent, and gurus who convince empty-headed celebrities that they are instant kabbalists.

We are not living in the generation of Abraham; we are living in the generation of Isaac. And so what can a decent person living in a generation like ours do? He or she can follow the example of Isaac and refuse to retreat. If we are not capable of establishing new frontiers of justice and culture, we can at least fight to preserve what has been entrusted to us by more creative and dynamic generations. We can redig the wells of our forebears.

Think back to the generations of East European Jews who, whether by choice or necessity, left behind the familiar, though often dangerous, patterns of Russia and Poland and crossed the seas to an unknown land, to the generations of grandparents or great-grandparents who, with the courage of the emigrant Abraham, braved the stormy North Atlantic, often in steerage, and arrived in a strange and bewildering land as greenhorns. They were exploited and shunned, often by the generation that preceded them, so that their children might "breathe free." Those generations had the audacity and faith to leap from the seventeenth to the twentieth century. With a fierce loyalty to Judaism and a passionate love for America, their *goldene medina*, they, in effect, turned the Statue of Liberty into the mezuzah on the "golden doors."

But ours is the generation of Isaac. We have been entrusted with a magnificent heritage of culture, social responsibility, and a love for learning and justice. Seemingly, we lack the mettle to expand that heritage, but do we have the loyalty and tenacity at least to preserve it, as did Isaac, for the next generation?

At this point, you might well ask, but wasn't Isaac a failure even as a father? Didn't he intend to give the blessing entrusted to him by Abraham to his crude and vulgar son, Esau? How would that have preserved the sacred heritage? And my response is to invite the reader to reconsider that well-known story in Genesis 27 that seemingly tells us how Rebekah tricked Isaac into giving the patriarchal blessing to Jacob. I believe that Isaac knew exactly what he was doing when he gave the blessing to his more deserving son. But first he had to determine that Jacob was, indeed, the more deserving son.

The text tells us that Isaac was old and that his eyesight was poor. It further tells us that he directed his older son, Esau, to go out and hunt some game for a ritual meal to precede the bestowal of the blessing. And it also tells us that Rebekah intervened so that her gentle, home-loving son, Jacob, dressed in Esau's gamey clothes, might receive the blessing. All of that is in our text, but what is *not* in the text is any suggestion that Isaac was foolish or senile or hard of hearing. In fact, when he entrusted the heritage to Jacob, it was with beautiful and inspiring words of blessing. And so what does that familiar text really tell us?

Isaac was faced with a dilemma. Tradition dictated that he bestow the patriarchal blessing upon his elder son. But he knew very well that Esau, who was courageous and virile, was also lacking in judgment and spirituality.

Hadn't Esau scorned and sloughed off his birthright for some bread and lentil stew? But what about his younger son? True, Jacob was wiser and certainly more gentle, but what about the virility and initiative of a young man who prefers to stay at home and indulge in cooking?

Isaac, meek and thoughtful, had gone through his entire life being compared to his dynamic father. And so when Isaac chose Esau for the blessing, not only was he conforming to the norm, but he was, in effect, also rejecting himself. He saw himself as inadequate, and he saw Jacob as a second Isaac. Bearing this in mind, let us now reexamine the text at the point where Jacob appears to Isaac disguised as Esau.

> *Jacob said to his father: "I am Esau, your first-born; I have done as you told me. Pray sit up and eat of the game, so that you may give me your blessing." And Isaac said to his son: "How did you succeed so quickly, my son?"*

Do you get the drift? Isaac was immediately aware of the deception. With the sharp hearing of a sight-impaired person, he heard the familiar voice of his son, Jacob, claiming to be Esau. And so he called his bluff, he asked Jacob how he managed to hunt down an animal so quickly. And what did Jacob answer? *"Because Adonai, your God, caused me good fortune."*

Remember, this was supposed to be Esau talking—Esau, the macho hunter; Esau who, when we last came upon him at a meal, *"ate, drank, got up, and left, and spurned his birthright"* (25:34). Not only did Isaac detect in Jacob's answer the familiar timbre of his voice, but he detected also the *language* of Jacob, the reverent words of a modest man. And so, quite naturally, the next verse has Isaac saying,

> *Come closer that I may feel you, my son, whether you are really my son Esau or not." So Jacob drew close to his father, Isaac, who said as he felt him, "The voice is the voice of Jacob but the hands are the hands of Esau."*

Jacob, of course, was wearing the animal skins that Rebekah had given him so that he should smell like Esau and so that his arms should be hairy like Esau's. And so Isaac felt the arms of the son whom he certainly already recognized as Jacob, and he cried out in wonder:

The voice is the voice of Jacob, but the hands are the hands of Esau!!

Isaac's initial surprise at feeling the hairiness of Esau on the arms of Jacob turned into a cry of joy. A miracle had happened! His fondest hope, his unutterable prayer, had been answered. The personality of Jacob had changed! From a docile, phlegmatic mama's boy—that is, from a clone of Isaac—had suddenly emerged a man of initiative, a man of action, an Abraham! Obviously, Jacob valued the patriarchal blessing so highly that he was willing to risk his life for it. He had no illusions about the wrath of Esau, the huntsman, once he discovered that his brother had stolen what was supposed to be his.

The gentle voice of Jacob was combined with the determined hands of Esau. Finally, Isaac realized, I have a son who is capable of carrying forward the courageous and pioneering quest for God initiated by my father, Abraham. Finally, Isaac could die in peace, his sacred task accomplished.

Turn 4

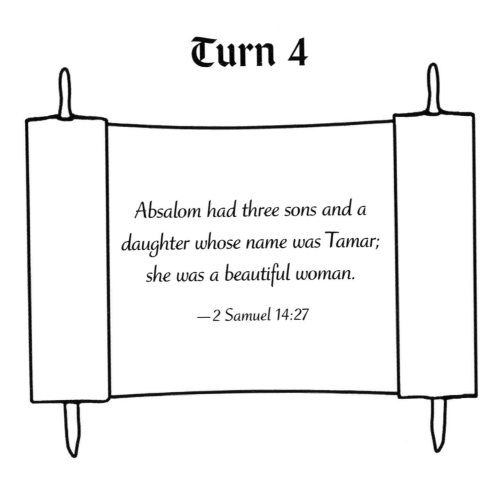

Absalom had three sons and a daughter whose name was Tamar; she was a beautiful woman.

—2 Samuel 14:27

We read in the second book of Samuel that Absalom, the fratricidal son of King David, returned to Jerusalem after a three-year exile to Geshur. The text goes on to describe his physical beauty and then to enumerate his progeny with this startling verse: *"Absalom had three sons and a daughter whose name was Tamar; she was a beautiful woman."* An obvious question: what were the names of Absalom's three sons? Most biblical genealogies mention only sons; this one not only names a daughter, very rare in itself, but it neglects to name the sons at all. One might take it for granted that Tamar is singled out by name because of a story about her that follows. But there *is* no story about her; she is never again mentioned! Tamar has the distinction of being the only person in the Bible described as beautiful with nothing further being said about her. She was "a beautiful woman"—that's it!

There is more, though, to pique the curiosity about Tamar, beginning with her name. What is there about the name Tamar that moved the biblical authors to assign it to three different women? The first Tamar was the daughter-in-law/inamorata of Judah (Gen. 38); the second Tamar was the ill-fated daughter of King David (2 Sam. 13); and the third was this beautiful daughter of Absalom about whom we know nothing.

The names of biblical characters are rarely replicated even once, and here we have the same name assigned to three distinct personalities. There was only one Abraham, one Sarah, one Moses, one Aaron, etc. One might expect to find repetitive names in particular among the kings, a David II or a Solomon III; after all, Egypt had Amenhotep IV and Rameses IX, and the Assyrians had Tiglath-Pileser III and Shalmaneser V. But no, the only names of Hebrew kings that are, in fact, replicated are Jeroboam, Jehoahaz, Joash, Shallum, and the second bearers of those names are virtually unknown except to Bible scholars. Not so the Tamars; there are full chapters with very poignant stories devoted to each of the first two. Is there, perhaps, something that links the three Tamars and that moved the biblical authors to bestow upon them that particular name?

The root meaning of the biblical Hebrew *tav-mem-resh* (as in *tamar* or *tomer*) is an erect object, in particular a palm tree. The form *timrah* is used by the prophet Joel (3:3) to indicate a pillar, and it is also used in one instance (Jer. 10:5) to indicate a polelike device used by farmers to frighten away predators. The date palm of the ancient Levant was the only common tree known to have been fertilized by men who collected the male flowers and then scattered the pollen over the fruit-bearing trees.

Clearly, the ancients, long before Freud, were aware of the sexual symbolism of the *t-m-r*, the date palm, or the erect column. One cannot help but wonder if the text of the book of Judges was not implying something about the extracurricular activities of the prophetess Deborah by stating that *"she used to sit under the palm* (tomer) *of Deborah"* where the Israelites would come to consult with her. But to return to our subject, I suggest that it is not coincidental that three women, all of whose stories indicate seductive sexuality or beauty, were named Tamar. Let's take a closer look at those stories.

I have been familiar with the story of the first Tamar ever since I was a nine-year-old Hebrew school student. We would spend an hour each day on the Torah portion of the week, and that brought us in December to the portion of *Va-yeshev*, Genesis 37-40. The story of Joseph and his brothers was familiar to us from the Bible stories that we had been taught in English since kindergarten, but in fourth grade we read through each of the Torah portions in the original Hebrew. When our teacher announced that chapter 38 was about something else, not important, and that we should turn to chapter 39 where the story of Joseph continued, I remembered that he had done the same thing back in October when we reached the final paragraph of Genesis 19. Skipping Torah passages was not lightly done in our Hebrew school and so, of course, when I got home I opened a copy of the English Bible and read the shocking story of the incestuous seduction of Lot by his two daughters.

I followed the same procedure with chapter 38 and was again shocked—*he spilled his seed on the ground*?! *"let me come in unto thee"*?! *"Tamar thy daughter-in-law hath played the harlot"*?! A story like that in the Torah?! I wondered, Do the goyim know that there is stuff like this in our Torah? As I grew older, I found other reasons to be fascinated by the study of the Bible; but for a nine-year-old, that was quite sufficient. A young woman, Tamar, was married to Judah's oldest son, Er, who died soon thereafter without an heir. Judah then directed his second son, Onan, to produce a child with Tamar who, according to levirate custom, would be considered the son of Er. The unwilling Onan then committed the dastardly act that qualified him for entry into the dictionary, and he was quickly dispatched. Custom then required that Judah's third son, Shelah, take responsibility for Tamar and produce a child with her for Er; but Judah, afraid of the effect of this femme fatale on his sons, deferred that liaison indefinitely.

Tamar then took matters into her own hands. She disguised herself (inventing a literary device that we find over and over again in Shakespeare and in classic opera) and set up as a prostitute at a place where she knew that her recently widowed father-in-law Judah would pass. He, as anticipated, solicited and then slept with her and she became pregnant. When informed of her pregnancy, Judah, as the head of his clan, sentenced her to death, but when she proved to him that he was the father of her child and that he was responsible for her neglect by Shelah, he pardoned her. She then gave birth to twins, one of whom, Perez, became the ancestor of King David.

We will turn to the story of Tamar II presently, but I want to digress here briefly to comment on King David, the towering heroic figure of biblical literature. He comes to mind immediately in any discussion of the three Tamars because he was a descendant of the first, the father of the second, and the grandfather of the third. It is as if the biblical authors were telling us to pay attention to any character by the name of Tamar because she will play a part in the heroic saga of King David. One cannot help but wonder, though, about the ancestry of that great king.

There are two women named in the Hebrew Bible as progenitrices of David and one additional woman in the Christian Bible, and all three add some blemish to his escutcheon. Tamar I, as we have noted, set herself up as a prostitute and although vindicated by Judah, their son Perez was the product not only of harlotry but also of incest. Blemish number one. The book of Ruth concludes by asserting that she and Boaz were the great-grandparents of David. Ruth, of course, was born a Moabite and as such, she was a member of a tribe forbidden to intermarry with Israel (see Deut. 23 and Neh. 13). Additionally, she was descended from the incestuous liaison between Lot and his older daughter. A second blot on the royal escutcheon!

For the third, we go to the Christian Bible's Gospel of Matthew. It opens with a rather problematic genealogy of Jesus which includes Rahab as the great-great-grandmother of David. Who was Rahab? She was the prostitute whose story is told in the second chapter of Joshua. (Rahab is worth a separate study; for whatever reasons, the Talmud [*Megillah* 14b and *Zevahim* 116b] rehabilitated her and had her marrying Joshua.) If we are to put any credence to these genealogies, the great King David was descended from two prostitutes and a forbidden Moabite, herself descended from an incestuous relationship. And of course, the royal line of David continued through his favored son, Solomon, the son of adulterers.

Tamar II was the daughter of King David by his wife, Maacah, also the mother of Absalom. Her tale of woe is told in 2 Samuel 13, not so much for its own sake but as a part of the story of the dynastic struggles among the sons of David that finally, after the deaths of Absalom and Amnon, ended with the coronation of Solomon. Who caused the deaths of the two leading contenders for the throne of Israel? Tamar II, at least indirectly and certainly through no fault of her own. And what is the first thing that we learn about Tamar ? *"Absalom son of David had a beautiful sister named Tamar."* Tamar II then, like her niece whom we meet a bit later in the narrative, is introduced as a beautiful woman. And then her half-brother Amnon comes onto the scene: *"And Amnon son of David became infatuated with her."* The plot thickens.

Amnon fell so deeply in love with Tamar that, recognizing that he could not have intimate relations with a half-sister, he became distraught and fell ill. David, the loving father (according to the Septuagint version of the story, Amnon was David's first and favored son), seeing how ill Amnon was, directed Tamar to care for him as Amnon had plotted with his cousin Jonadab. Once Amnon had Tamar in his house, he coaxed her to lie with him, but she answered, *"Don't, brother. Don't force me. Such things are not done in Israel! Don't do such a vile thing!"* Clearly, she was innocent although just a verse later, attempting to put Amnon off, she added, *"Please speak to the king; he will not refuse me to you."* Amnon, though, refused to be put off and *"he overpowered her and lay with her by force."* In simple language, he raped her.

It is interesting to speculate on what Tamar meant when she urged Amnon to speak to the king. It is clear that she knew that relations between a brother and sister were "not done in Israel" and so why speak to the king? One school of thought suggests that she was playing for time, looking desperately for some way to forestall Amnon so that she could get safely out of his house. But another school has it that she did, in fact, reciprocate Amnon's love and thought that their father might find some solution for them. After all, hadn't their father broken the seventh commandment with Bathsheba and survived? But whichever interpretation one chooses, it is clear that Amnon raped Tamar and then proceeded to do even worse: *"Then Amnon felt a great loathing for her; indeed, his loathing for her was greater than the passion that he had felt for her. And Amnon said to her, 'Get out!' She pleaded with him . . . but he would not listen to her."* Amnon was an unmitigated cad, certainly one of the most unsympathetic characters in the entire Bible.

Tamar left Amnon's house in great distress, *"screaming loudly as she went,"* and took refuge in the home of her brother, Absalom. That, of course, exacerbated the enmity between the rivals Amnon and Absalom and, after biding his time waiting for the opportune moment, Absalom conspired to have Amnon murdered. That led to Absalom's banishment from the royal court, and while there was a brief reconciliation between David and the leading claimant to his throne, it ultimately led to Absalom's armed rebellion against David and his murder by David's general, Joab. It was during the brief reconciliation between Absalom and his father and before his nearly successful rebellion, that we read of the birth of his three sons *"and a daughter whose name was Tamar; she was a beautiful woman."*

As mentioned above, we know nothing at all about this Tamar, the one whom we refer to as Tamar III. But what can we surmise? I believe that the brief mention of this third Tamar was intended by the author to alert us to something about the house of David and to underscore the relationship of David to the women in his orbit. If we know nothing at all about her other than that she was beautiful, why mention her name at all, especially in the absence of the names of her three brothers?

I believe that naming his daughter Tamar was one of the methods chosen by the rebellious Absalom to debase his father and win over the sympathy of the people. It was a way of reminding the people that the old king was a descendant of prostitution and incest—Tamar I—and the foolish father who put his daughter in harm's way, Tamar II. Did Absalom really feel that he had to debase his father in order to buttress his claim to the throne? That is clear from his compliance with the advice of one his counselors, Ahitophel.

Ahitopel, formerly a member of David's court, joined Absalom after David was forced to flee from Jerusalem.

> *Ahitophel said to Absalom: "Have intercourse with your father's concubines, whom he left to mind the palace; and when all Israel hears that you have dared the wrath of your father, all who support you will be encouraged." So . . . Absalom lay with his father's concubines before the eyes of all Israel.* (2 Sam. 16:21ff)

This is, *mirabile dictu*, the same Absalom whose death was so grievously lamented by David: "*O my son, my son Absalom! If only I had died instead of you! O Absalom, my son, my son!*" (2 Sam. 19:1)

This story is reminiscent of ancient Greek and Egyptian mythologies where we read of usurpers solidifying their claims to the throne by appropriating the wives or concubines of the rulers whom they are attempting to supplant. A variation appears again in the story of the Davidic succession when, after the accession of Solomon to the throne, his rival older brother Adonijah asked for permission to marry Abishag, David's last concubine (1 Kings 2: 13ff). That request, recognized immediately by Solomon as an attempt to overthrow him, was swiftly punished by execution.

Was there actually a third Tamar? Or was she, perhaps, the invention of a clever author attempting to derogate King David, possibly a descendant of Absalom or of Saul or a member of the royal court of the Northern Kingdom after the rebellion against David's grandson, Rehoboam? There was no shortage of people eager to besmirch the memory of David in the generations immediately following his death, the generations when the stories that made their ways into our Bible were being collected.

Several generations later, the prophets, particularly Isaiah and Jeremiah, tended to idealize the mythic reign of David, possibly because of the corruption that they saw in the royal courts of their times. Subsequently, David evolved into the psalmist, "the sweet singer of Israel," the paragon king, and the source of messianic hope. But always, lurking in the background of his legend, were the three Tamars.

Turn 5

*You stand this day, all of you,
before Adonai, your God.*

—Deuteronomy 29:9

On a Saturday night in the '80s, I joined my father at the home of friends for a *melaveh malkah* (a gathering to prolong the spirit of Shabbat after *Havdalah* by singing, eating, drinking, and exchanging ideas inspired by Torah). Several of the guests offered passages from Torah, proceeded to interpret them, and received the traditional *Yishar kohakha* (May your strength increase!) from the other attendees, though most of their interpretations were rather pedestrian. One of the guests, though, offered a beautiful example of the process of midrash (playing with the words in such a way as to find lessons which may or may not have been intended in the original text), which I decided deserved further amplification. I credit him (Baruch Duvdevani of Jerusalem, *a'h*), with the terse original midrash, and I hope that I honor his memory by presenting it with my own "variations on a theme." Thus does the venerable process of midrash continue to flourish.

The book of Deuteronomy consists of three great orations by Moses to the people of Israel before his death. The third oration (chap. 11:26; 28:69) is followed by a final dramatic appeal to the people to live up to their covenant with God. In order to speak to the hearts of every one of the people of Israel individually, Moses began his appeal with these words:

> *You stand this day, all of you, before Adonai your God—your tribal heads, your elders, and your officials, all the men of Israel, your children, your wives, even the stranger within your camp, from your wood chopper to your water drawer—to enter into the covenant of Adonai your God and its sanctions, which Adonai your God is concluding with you this day, so that He may establish you this day as His people and be your God, as He promised you and as He swore to your fathers, to Abraham, Isaac and Jacob.* (29:9-12)

What a magnificent scene! All the people were assembled—and it is interesting to note that, contrary to most covenantal formulations in the Torah, this one included women and children—to voice their assent. Nobody was excluded from the *berit*; it included everybody *"from your wood chopper to your water drawer."*

But wait a minute! Who is included in that continuum from wood chopper to water drawer? That is tantamount to saying, in contemporary language, "from ditchdigger to garbageman." It includes only the most menial level of society, not the gamut which we might infer from the context. One might have expected the text to read "from your prince to your wood chopper and from your priest to your water drawer." How many Israelites could possibly have been subsumed in as debased a category as wood chopper to water drawer?

I am by no means the first student of Torah to recognize that this phraseology is problematic. Rashi, the most widely read of all the classic Bible commentators (France, eleventh century), considered the wood choppers and the water drawers to refer back to the *ger*, the stranger, of the previous phrase. He opined, "This teaches us that certain Canaanites came as proselytes in the days of Moses." Rashi, taking his cue from a story about the Gibeonites in the book of Joshua, suggested that Moses made these proselytes into wood choppers and water drawers as Joshua later did with the Gibeonites who attached themselves to Israel. (That text in Joshua 9 refers to wood choppers and water drawers three times.)

With all due respect to Rashi, I find this interpretation unacceptable. To identify the *ger*, "the stranger within your camp" who stands with the rest of Israel, prepared to enter into the eternal covenant with motley pagans pressed into servitude is to deny all those great passages in the Torah that refer to the *ger* in benign terms, as for example, "*The* ger *who dwells with you shall be treated as a native, and you shall love him as yourself*" (Lev. 19:34; also Num. 9:14; Deut. 10:19; etc.). No, there is a strong disjunctive accent, *etnah*, in the traditional text separating the "stranger within your camp" from the hewers and the drawers. The climactic "from your wood chopper to your water drawer" is clearly meant to summarize all those mentioned previously; it is meant to include the entire people of Israel without exception.

Other commentators, notably Sforno (Italy, sixteenth century) and Malbim (Poland, nineteenth century), also felt that there was something wrong with the wood chopper-water drawer formulation. Sforno recognized that it must indicate a gamut of some kind, and so he suggested that it meant from the foremost among the wood choppers to the least of the water drawers, while Malbim, differing with Rashi, denied that they were related to the strangers. He suggested that the formulation indicated an inferior category of people, not included among the aforementioned. I cannot accept any of these interpretations, and I cite them only to indicate that commentators throughout the ages have had trouble with this strange formulation.

I have no doubt that the author was attempting to underscore the idea that the divine *berit* extended even to the lowliest citizens of the Israelite community, even to the wood choppers and the water drawers, and that somehow, either by an infelicitous choice of prepositions or a clumsy redaction, we were left with what appears to be a gamut but is, in fact, a very narrow slice of society. And that, of course, invites speculation. Thus begins the process of midrash.

One of the most impressive elements of the passage in Deuteronomy 29 is that Moses's dramatic charge is addressed not only to the generation of the wilderness but also the generations of Israel yet unborn.

> *I make this covenant with its sanctions not with you alone but both*
> *with those who are standing with us this day before Adonai our God*
> *and with those who are not with us this day.* (29:13-14)

In other words, the *berit* is eternal; it is as much binding on the Jews of the twenty-first century as it was upon the Jews addressed personally by Moses before his death millennia ago. And not only was Israel of the *future* included in the *berit* but also Israel of the past, going back to the generation of Abraham. The *berit* was intended for all the *people* of Israel and all the *generations* of Israel. That it was intended for all the *people* of Moses's generation is clear from the word *kulkhem* (all of you) followed by the specific references to tribal heads, elders, officers, men, women, children, and strangers in verses 9 and 10a; that it was intended for all the *generations*, past and future, is midrashically clear from that problematic formulation "*from your wood chopper to your water drawer,*" in verse 10b. How so?

Who was the first wood chopper in Jewish history? The answer is obvious: the first Jew, Abraham. When did Abraham chop wood? At the most difficult moment of his life, preparing for that horrendous test of faith that we call the *akedah*, we read,

> *Early next morning, Abraham saddled his ass and took with him*
> *two of his servants and his son Isaac. He split the wood for the burnt*
> *offering, and he set out for the place of which God had told him.*
> (Gen. 22:3ff)

That the wood chopped by Abraham was not incidental to the story is attested by the fact that it is mentioned four more times in the next few verses:

> *Abraham took the wood for the burnt offering and put it on his son*
> *Isaac . . . And he [Isaac] said: "Here are the firestone and the wood,*
> *but where is the sheep for the offering?" . . . Abraham built an altar*
> *there; he laid out the wood; he bound his son Isaac; he laid him on the*
> *altar, on top of the wood.*

The faith even unto death of Abraham was proven on Mount Moriah. But before setting out for Moriah, we are told that, even with two servants available, Abraham himself split the wood. And as if to emphasize that fact, the wood is mentioned four more times. And so we find the first Jew, at the most crucial moment of his life, chopping wood.

We can easily identify Abraham as the *first* Jew, but who will be the *last* Jew? That might seem like a difficult or even a frightening question, but actually, tradition is quite clear on the matter. Who is God supposed to send to announce "the end of days"?

> *Lo, I will send the prophet Elijah to you before the coming of the*
> *awesome, fearful day of Adonai.* (Mal. 3:23)

Jewish tradition has, ever since the Babylonian exile, identified Elijah as the precursor of the Messiah. It is he who is supposed to announce finally that the task of the Jewish people has come to an end because then even non-Jews will *"attach themselves to Adonai . . . and [God's] House shall be called a house of prayer for all peoples"* (Isa. 56:6-7). It is on our Feast of Redemption, Passover, that we feel the presence of Elijah most palpably. Celebrants hail his anticipated arrival by imbibing a fifth cup, the cup of messianic redemption, the Cup of Elijah. (See Turn 20 re Elijah.). The tradition that Elijah will prefigure the Messiah is neatly summed up in the *Pesikta Rabbati* (a medieval Palestinian collection of homilies):

Three days before the coming of the Messiah, Elijah will appear on the mountains of Israel and cry: "O Mountains of Israel, how long will you remain waste and desolate?" Then he will proclaim world peace . . . And the Holy One will . . . redeem Israel.

Now if Abraham, the first Jew, was a wood chopper, is it possible that Elijah, who will announce the end of Jewish history, was a water drawer? And might there actually be some connection between water drawing and the onset of the Messianic Age? The answer to both questions is yes.

Just as Abraham, at the most dramatic juncture of his life, chopped wood for a momentous sacrifice, so Elijah, at a parallel moment of high drama, drew water for a sacrifice. The scene was Mount Carmel where Elijah challenged *"the four hundred and fifty prophets of Baal and the four hundred prophets of Asherah"* who served Queen Jezebel (1 Kings 18:19). After the hundreds of pagan prophets failed in their attempts to coax fire from the heavens to consume their sacrifices, it was Elijah's turn. He invited all of the Israelite spectators to gather around him, and he rebuilt an old altar that had been dedicated to the worship of Adonai. But then, instead of simply laying out his sacrifice and calling on God to send down fire, he dug a large trench around the altar and he instructed the spectators:

"Fill four jars with water and pour it over the burnt offering and the wood." Then he said, "Do it a second time;" and they did it a second time. "Do it a third time," he said; and they did it a third time. The water ran down around the altar, and even the trench was filled with water.

Notice the correspondence between the four mentions of the wood in rapid succession in the Abraham story and the four jars of water in the Elijah story. Notice also that while Jewish tradition assigns the reading of the *Akedah* to Rosh Ha-Shanah, it assigns Elijah's cry of victory, *"Adonai, He is God! Adonai, He is God!"* to the conclusion of Yom Kippur. And just in case anyone misses the connection when Elijah's shout issues from the throats of the congregants, it is followed immediately by a blast of the shofar, bringing us back to the ram caught by its horns in the thicket and sacrificed by Abraham in place of Isaac. These texts are intimately connected, and we are reminded of that connection every year on our most sacred days.

Readers will readily concede that Abraham, the wood chopper, was the first Jew but they might never have thought of Elijah as the last Jew. Even if they are willing to concede that the Malachi prophecy and many later rabbinic teachings indicate explicitly that Elijah will proclaim the Messianic Age, they might demur and point out that Elijah's confrontation and his water drawing on Mount Carmel had nothing to do with the "end of days." But the connection between water drawing and the Messianic Age is not at all tenuous. It is as explicit as can be in one of the most beautiful messianic passages in the Bible:

> *Behold the God who gives me triumph!*
> *I am confident, unafraid;*
> *For Yah Adonai is my strength and might,*
> *And He has been my deliverance.*
> *Joyfully shall you draw water*
> *From the fountains of triumph.* (Isa. 12:2-3)

If there are any doubts about the messianic context of these verses, I remind the reader that it is both preceded and followed by the standard apocalyptic formula "*bayom hahu* (in that day)" (11:10, 11:11, 12:1, and 12:4). In the day that Malachi called "*the awesome, fearful day of Adonai*," Elijah will once again invite us to "*draw water from the fountains of triumph.*" It is of interest that that messianic passage from Isaiah opens the Saturday evening Havdalah service and that folk tradition prescribes the singing of *Eliyahu Ha-Navi* (Elijah, the Prophet) at the end of Havdalah.

And so Jewish history began with a hero who chopped wood at a moment of high drama in his life and it will conclude with a hero who drew water at his moment of high drama. All the people of Israel and all the generations of Israel, including those as yet unborn, are partners in the eternal *berit* with God. From the days of Abraham, the wood chopper, until Elijah, the water drawer, returns to proclaim the Messianic Age, it is the duty of every Jew to work as a partner with God. Then,

> *Adonai your God will bring you to the land that your fathers possessed,*
> *and you shall possess it. And He will make you more prosperous and*
> *more numerous than your fathers. Then Adonai your God will open up*
> *your heart and the hearts of your offspring to love Adonai your God with*
> *all your heart and soul, in order that you may live.* (Deut. 30:5-6)

Turn 6

And Samuel cut Agag down before Adonai at Gilgal.

—1 Samuel 15:33

There is certainly a lot of cruelty and bloodshed recorded in the Bible, but the distinguished theologian Martin Buber was particularly repelled by the story of the vengeful slaying of the Amalekite king Agag by Samuel. It was not just that Samuel killed one more Amalekite; a few verses earlier we read that God had commanded Saul to kill all the Amalekites, *"men and women, infants and sucklings, oxen and sheep, camels and asses"* (15:3). Saul chose, for whatever reason, to spare Agag. But then Samuel came to the camp of the Israelite army and interrupted the victory celebration by berating Saul for allowing some of the animals to be taken as booty and for allowing Agag to survive.

It was not so much Samuel's killing of Agag that bothered Buber; Agag was, after all, only one out of thousands already killed. It was, rather, the reason given for the killing, that God wanted the death of every Amalekite, not just the soldiers but the women and infants as well. God, according to the text, had commanded the total slaughter of the Amalekites. Because Saul had seen fit to spare one person, Samuel informed him that *"Adonai has this day torn the kingship of Israel away from you."* And then the text makes it clear that Samuel did not simply slay Agag, but he cut him down (or, in other translations, hewed him in pieces; the meaning of the Hebrew *va-y'shasef* is not clear) *"before Adonai,"* that is, in fulfillment of God's command.

I can well understand why Buber and so many others to this very day are sickened by that story and by similar stories of gratuitous barbarity in the book that is supposed to be the fountainhead of our faith. Some turn their backs on the Bible, and on God, citing those all too numerous passages that describe a god of vengeance and wrath. The young Buber too was moving in that direction. He tells the story of his crisis of faith in an autobiographical fragment entitled "Samuel and Agag." During his student days, he was riding on a train and by chance shared a compartment with a learned old Orthodox

Jew. They began discussing the problems inherent in certain biblical texts, and Buber said that he was very troubled by God's commanding Saul to kill all the Amalekites; "I have never been able to believe that this is a message of God. I do not believe it."

Buber then goes on to describe the reaction of the older man to his declaration of disbelief:

> "So? You do not believe it?" "No," I answered, "I do not believe it." "What do you believe then?" "I believe," I replied without reflecting, "that Samuel has misunderstood God." And he again slowly, but more softly than before: "So? You believe that?" And I: "Yes." Then we were both silent. But now something happened the like of which I have rarely seen before or since in this very long life. The angry countenance opposite me became transformed . . . "Well," said the man with a positively gentle tender clarity, "I think so too." (*Autobiographical Fragments*, pp. 31-33)

And then Buber commented, "An observant Jew . . . when he has to choose between God and the Bible, chooses God." What a magnificent declaration of faith—faith in the God of whom Moses sang, *"His deeds are perfect, yea, all His ways are just"* (Deut. 32:4). Again, **"An observant Jew . . . when he has to choose between God and the Bible, chooses God."**

Martin Buber understood, as all who truly love God and love scripture should understand, that those who recorded and preserved our sacred texts were human beings, fallible people who occasionally may have misunderstood the intent. The word may emanate from the infinite God, but it comes to us through the cerebral filters and the hands of finite mortals. Buber again:

> Misunderstanding has again and again attached itself to understanding; the manufactured has been mixed with the received. We have no objective criterion for the distinction; we have only faith—when we have it. Nothing can make me believe in a God who punishes Saul because he did not murder his enemy.

The person of faith, the one who believes in and loves God and humanity, must resolve for him/herself the tension between the word of God and the word of God's human expositors. No easy task. And so the question: Did

Samuel indeed kill Agag at the command of God? Or is it possible that a zealous scribe, who might have had very good reasons for despising the memory of a cruel Amalekite king, took it for granted that Samuel would have hacked Agag into pieces? Let's begin our search for an answer to that question by looking at the connection between our story and the holiday of Purim.

The story of Saul, Samuel, and Agag is read each year in the synagogue on the Sabbath before the holiday of Purim, *Shabbat Zakhor* (the Sabbath of "Remember"). It is so named because of the brief passage from Deuteronomy 25 that provides a link between the Torah and the much later text for Purim, the book of Esther. Haman, the archvillain who wanted to murder all the Jews of Persia, is referred to in Esther as *Agagi*, which is understood to mean "a descendant of Agag." The text in Deuteronomy decrees that the Israelites should never forget that the Amalekites *"surprised you on the march when you were famished and weary, and cut down all the stragglers in your rear . . . Do not forget!"* (Deut. 25:17ff) Agag, as we have seen, was the name of the king of the Amalekites in the days of Saul and Samuel, but there is a brief allusion to Agag also in the book of Numbers (24:7) that might indicate that the Amalekite king in the days of Moses had the same name. And so the Amalekites and Agag were the eternal enemies of the Jews, and Haman, according to the traditions surrounding the otherwise joyful holiday of Purim, was the evil incarnation of Amalek and Agag.

One of the longstanding customs of the holiday of Purim is the imbibing of intoxicating beverages, often to excess. According to the text at the conclusion of the book of Esther, following the downfall of Haman, Mordecai decreed a day of "feasting and merrymaking." This "feasting and merrymaking," repeated twice in chapter 9, is an echo of the opening the book, where we find King Ahasuerus presiding over a feast where *"royal wine was served in abundance."* And so that there be no misunderstanding about what the text means by *"in abundance,"* the next verse reads, *"And the rule for the drinking was, 'No restrictions!'"* (Est. 1:8). And then we read that as a result of his drunkenness, the king ordered his queen Vashti to display her beauty before the besotted crowd. She refused; she was summarily deposed. And that, of course, led to the selection of Esther as the new queen.

The customs of the holiday of Purim, including drinking, are discussed in the Talmud in the tractate *Megillah*. Among those customs, Rava (fourth-century Babylonian sage) taught, *"It is the duty of a person to drink so much on Purim that he cannot tell the difference between cursed be Haman and blessed be Mordecai"* (*Megillah* 7b). (It should be noted that long before the days of gender sensitivity, the Jerusalem Talmud added this variant after Haman and Mordecai: "cursed be Zeresh and blessed be Esther.")

After recording the opinion of Rava that the proper observance of Purim includes drunkenness, the Talmud goes on to relate the following rather bizarre story:

> *Rabbah and Rabbi Zera (fourth-century Babylonian sages) joined together in a Purim feast [seudat Purim]. They got drunk, and Rabbah arose and killed [lit. cut the throat of] R. Zera. On the next day he prayed for mercy, and Rabbi Zera revived.*

That's the brief text that I want to examine more closely, but for those who might think that the sages of the Talmud lacked senses of humor, I will add just the next two lines:

> *The next year [Rabbah] said: "Sir, shall we get together for the Purim feast again?" [Rabbi Zera] answered: "One cannot depend on the regular occurrence of miracles."*

Rabbah killed Rabbi Zera?! We are talking about two of the great sages of fourth-century Babylonia, sages whose opinions are recorded over and over again in rabbinic literature! The idea that a great teacher of Torah like Rabbah would act like a drunken hooligan was so inconceivable to a seventeenth-century Venetian rabbi, Azariah Figo, that he devoted one of his published sermons to a minute analysis of the story. Azariah Figo was by no means a liberal interpreter of Jewish law; he was quite conservative and is still accepted as an important authority in halachic circles. The sermon that I refer to may be found in his most important book, *Binah L'Ittim*, published in Venice in 1648.

Figo begins his sermon by noting that we have certain rituals to remind us of God's miracles, for example, the eating of matzah and maror on Passover. But he has difficulty accepting the teaching of Rava that it is a religious obligation to drink wine to excess in order to celebrate Purim properly.

How is it possible, writes Figo, to establish a celebration and the remembrance of God's miracle on the kind of drunkenness that would cause a person to lose the powers of common sense and judgment which are the essence of our humanity, the kind of drunkenness that can lead to injury?

Figo then goes on to examine at great length the story in the book of Esther about the rise of the wicked Haman to high rank in the court of King Ahasuerus and the fall of Mordecai the Jew to such low standing that even after he saves the king's life, his deed is forgotten. (I must note here parenthetically that critical scholars have long considered the book of Esther to be a work of fiction, possibly written to explain the existence of a popular holiday celebrated since ancient times by Persian Jews. It was probably because the author knew that he was writing a popular romance that the name of God does not appear in the book of Esther. Figo, though, treats the book as historical fact in his sermon.)

According to Figo, the lots that Haman cast to set the date on which he would dispose of Mordecai were meant to determine when Mordecai's *mazal* (astrological sign) would be bad and his own *mazal* good. What, then, was the great miracle of the book of Esther? God abrogated both sets of omens, both Mordecai's and Haman's, for that day. And so Jews must use the day of Purim to examine every aspect of that great miracle in order to understand the extent of God's providence. A person whose head is beclouded by excessive drinking will not be able to comprehend the rise of Haman and the fall of Mordecai, followed by the fall of Haman and the rise of Mordecai. His brain will get so muddled by all the drinking that finally he will not be able to tell the difference between "cursed be Haman and blessed be Mordecai."

And so, writes Figo, how do we fulfill the obligation of drinking on Purim? Certainly not to the extent of drunkenness which is absolutely unlike the eating of matzah and maror on Passover. Eating those symbolic foods is intended precisely to *increase* our understanding of God's miraculous intervention in Egypt. But drunkenness on Purim would *decrease* our understanding of God's intervention with the *mazalot* of Haman and Mordecai, and so that certainly cannot be Rava's intention. Rather, Figo taught, Rava was teaching that we should celebrate Purim with feasting and drinking, but drinking just up to that point when the distinction between "cursed be Haman" and "blessed be

Mordecai" begins to blur. That should be our sobriety test: when we begin mixing up Haman and Mordecai, that is the signal to stop drinking.

Having made that clear, Figo then returns to the incident of the killing of Rabbi Zera. According to Figo, Rabbah did not physically kill Rabbi Zera. Rather, as they were arguing the more abstruse points of the ascent of Haman and the descent of Mordecai and then the descent of Haman and the ascent of Mordecai, and the abrogation of their *mazalot* by God, Rabbah destroyed Rabbi Zera intellectually. As they continued drinking wine and arguing about the text, Rabbah became more and more vehement and Zera became more and more confused until Rabbah totally and embarrassingly demolished Zera.

The next day, according to Figo's reconstruction of the story, Rabbah felt so bad about the way that he had treated his friend, Rabbi Zera, that he went to his home and apologized. Rabbah's apology revived Rabbi Zera's spirits but not so thoroughly that he was willing to take the chance of being similarly demolished and embarrassed the next year.

And so what have we learned from Azariah Figo's sermon? Three things, and these are:

1. that in order to celebrate Purim properly, we must carefully consider all of the details of the book of Esther, in particular the relative positions of Haman and Mordecai;
2. that while it is clear that we are obliged to drink more than usual at our Purim celebration, the limit of that mitzvah is the point at which we become confused by the text; and, most important for the purposes of this essay,
3. that an ancient text that states, clearly and unambiguously, "Rabbah arose and killed Rabbi Zera," does not mean that at all; it means that Rabbah overwhelmed Zera in argumentation and embarrassed him.

Thus did Azariah Figo, an authoritative and strict interpreter of Jewish law, reject the clear meaning of a sacred text. Why? Because it offended his ethical sensibilities. And so we return now to the ethical sensibilities of Martin Buber who also rejected the clear meaning of a sacred text. What was Buber's rationale? "An observant Jew . . . when he has to choose between God and the Bible, chooses God." And if the reader is troubled by my comparing a

Talmudic text to a biblical text, one should understand that Jewish tradition considers the writings of the ancient rabbis to be the "Oral Torah," the sacred elucidation and expansion of the original "Written Torah." Both are considered sacred.

And so here we have two texts, one biblical and one Talmudic, that tell the stories of two murders, the first the murder of Agag by Samuel and the second the murder of Rabbi Zera by Rabbah. Are these stories true? No, I reject them utterly because I believe that a truly religious person, a true lover of God, has the obligation to reject a sacred text if his intellect and his ethical sensibilities tell him that that text diminishes God, that it is, in fact, an affront to God. Buber refused to believe that God ordered Saul to destroy the entire Amalekite people, "men and women, infants and sucklings." Azariah Figo refused to believe that it is a mitzvah to get so drunk on Purim that one might kill a dear friend. In both cases, they refused to believe a sacred text because they believed more deeply in God.

All too often those students of Torah who approach a text with a critical eye are made to feel that they are somehow less reverent and less faithful than students who are so in awe of the text that they suspend their critical faculties. It is important to reject that kind of thinking or lack of thinking. Students of Torah should be rigorous in their demand that each and every text truly reflect the will of God, the God who commanded us that we should be holy as God is holy. If our God-given minds make it impossible for us to conceive of God commanding Saul to kill women and infants or to conceive of God commanding us to get so drunk on Purim that we might be capable of murder, then we are not *less* reverent; we are *more* reverent.

A truly observant Jew who has to choose between a time-hallowed text and God will choose God, the God whom he or she can believe in, humbly imitate, and teach to the next generation. "*This is my God, and I will glorify Him!*" (Exod. 15:2).

Turn 7

Tell me all the wonderful things that Elisha has done.

—2 Kings 8:4

I have often heard fellow Jews heap scorn on the Christian Bible as a collection of fairy tales. "How," they ask, "can an intelligent person believe that nonsense?" "What nonsense?" I ask. And the reply invariably has to do with the miracles that the Gospels ascribe to Jesus. "Am I supposed to believe that Jesus cured people by touching them? That he fed multitudes with a couple of fish and a few loaves? That he walked on water? That he rose from the dead? *Bobbeh mayses!* (Old wives' tales)."

"Well," I ask naively. "What about all the miracles ascribed to Moses and Elijah and Elisha? They're all in *our* Bible. Do you believe them?"

"How can you make such a comparison?" my favorite scorner responds in an offended tone. "Those are ancient traditions, the words of God and the prophets. You don't ask questions about such things."

The eminent psychologist, Theodore Reik, once told the story of a little boy who was spending the night at the house of an aunt. As she put him to bed, he complained when she shut the light. The aunt asked, "What's the matter with you? You always sleep in the dark at home." And he answered, "Yes, Auntie, but that's my own dark." So too with Bible stories; people seem to prefer their own dark.

The belief in miracles was a major part of Judaism in the biblical period, and it was certainly an important element in the days of the Talmud and Midrash. There were, however, dissenters among the classical rabbis. In one of the most amazing (and, I believe, intentionally humorous) passages in the Talmud, Rabbi Eliezer (second century) invoked a series of miracles to prove that his interpretation of a law was correct and that the interpretation of his colleagues was wrong (*Baba Metzia* 59b). When heaven itself intervened, declaring that Rabbi Eliezer was correct, Rabbi Joshua rebuked the heavenly voice, saying, in effect, that discussions of law among the sages were not the business of heaven. Commenting on this well-known story, Rabbi Jeremiah (third century) formulated a principle that might well serve as the motto of all those future generations that would have to deal with miracle stories: *Ein anu mashgihin b'vat kol* (We do not pay any heed to a heavenly voice). And a passage in the tractate *Yevamot* (121b) teaches that miracles may not be cited to prove anything.

Although there was a certain amount of skepticism among the early sages about miracles in their own times, there is no doubt that, in general, they accepted the miracle traditions that are found in the pages of Jewish scripture. They believed that miracles ceased with the passing of the age of prophecy, but unlike Maimonides, the great twelfth-century rationalist, they were not bothered by the miracles in the Bible.

I find it very revealing that the medieval rabbis who chose the various prophetic texts that we call haftarot to complement the weekly Torah portions chose a miracle story as the haftarah that follows the reading of the portion *Va-yera* (Gen. 18-22). Whenever possible, the rabbis chose haftarot that would remind the worshiper of something in the Torah portion. The portion of *Va-yera* has in it several stories that the rabbis might have chosen to underscore by their choice of a haftarah, Abraham's hospitality to the three heavenly messengers, his bargaining with God for the people of Sodom, the infatuation of King Abimelech for Sarah, Sarah's jealousy and the consequent expulsion of Hagar, or the most dramatic, Abraham's intended sacrifice of Isaac. But what did the rabbis, in fact, choose to highlight? The rabbis went for the miracle story, the pregnancy of Sarah in old age.

What prophetic reading did they choose as the haftarah? The story in 2 Kings 4 which tells, among other things, of the miraculous pregnancy of a Shunemite woman. Elisha rewarded this generous but barren woman with the birth of a son. And just as Sarah found it difficult to believe that she was capable of child bearing, so did the Shunemite woman plead with Elisha, after the annunciation: "Please, my lord, man of God, do not delude your maidservant." (2 Kings 4:16)

That particular haftarah has in it three separate miracle stories: first, the reward of an endless supply of oil for a debt-ridden woman; second, the birth mentioned above; and third, the reviving of a dead child. All three of these miracles, as well as others performed by Elisha, are retold in the Christian Bible, as is also the annunciation of miraculous birth. There are numerous examples of miraculous births in the Jewish Bible—Isaac's, Samson's, Samuel's, and their annunciations by angels or prophets. Those annunciations are echoed in the Christian Bible's Gospel of Luke chapter 1 twice; the angel Gabriel reveals not only the forthcoming miraculous birth of Jesus but also the birth of John to the aged Elizabeth.

Of all the miracle workers in the Jewish Bible, Elisha was certainly the most prolific and the text in 2 Kings makes it quite clear that he was widely recognized as such. Even the king Jehoram was aware of Elisha's reputation and so he summoned Elisha's servant, Gehazi, and asked him:

> *"Tell me all the wonderful things that Elisha has done." While he was telling the king how [Elisha] revived a dead person* . . . (2 Kings 8:4-5)

That particular telling was interrupted by the appearance of the Shunemite woman mentioned above, but Elisha's catalogue of miracles, as recorded in the book of 2 Kings, included all of these:

— Witnessing the miraculous ascent of Elijah (2:11-12)
— Splitting the Jordan River (2:14)
— Purifying lethal water (2:21)
— Causing bears to kill nasty boys (2:24)
— Divining the forthcoming defeat of Moab (3:16-19)
— Producing abundant oil for a poor woman (4:3-4)
— Rewarding a barren woman with a son (4:16)
— Reviving that dead son (4:32-35)
— Purifying a lethal stew (4:40-41)
— Multiplying loaves of bread for a multitude (4:42-44)
— Curing the leper Naaman (5:1-14)
— Punishing the venal Gehazi with leprosy (5:27)
— Causing an ax head to float (6:5-6)
— Foreseeing the actions of the king of Aram (6:9-12)
— Calling down blindness on the army of Aram (6:18)
— Prophesying the rout of the Aramean army (7)
— Prophesying the accession of Hazael as king of Aram (8:13-15)

— Prophesying the fall of the House of Ahab and the death of Jezebel (9:1-10)
— Prophesying, on his deathbed, King Joash's victory over Aram (13:14-19)
— Even after death, reviving a dead man whose corpse touched his own (13:21)

I can well imagine contemporaries of the Gospel writers paraphrasing King Jehoram's request to Gehazi: "Tell us all of the wonderful things that Jesus has done" and the writers then going to the book of 2 Kings and appropriating the popular Elisha stories for their own purposes. It was at the very same time that the Gospel writers were ascribing Elisha's miracles to Jesus that the rabbis were asserting that the age of miracles was over. But there was no major voice in that classical rabbinic period that ever denied that miracles did occur in biblical times.

It was not until the twelfth century that an authoritative Jewish voice raised doubts about biblical miracles. Maimonides did not actually deny that those miracles took place; rather he rationalized them as natural occurrences at the right time and place. In his *Mishneh Torah*, he asserted that Moses established his greatness not by the performance of miracles but rather by the revelation of God's law at Sinai. But Maimonides's skepticism did not, by any means, put an end to the belief in miracles among Jews. Just a few decades later, Nahmanides, the leading Spanish scholar of his day, opined that no one could claim to accept the Torah if he denied the miracles recorded in it.

And so the argument persists down to our own day with liberal religionists, both Christian and Jewish, de-emphasizing the miraculous and focusing on the ethical in scripture, while the fundamentalists insist, echoing God's rebuke to Sarah, "*Is anything too wonderful for Adonai?*" Fundamentalists might remind us that when Moses expressed skepticism about God's ability to provide meat for the entire people of Israel in the wilderness, God replied sternly, "*Is there any limit to Adonai's power? You shall soon see whether what I have said happens or not.*" And then followed the miracle of the quail (Num. 11:21-34). What, then, can we say about miracles? Do the miracle stories in both the Jewish and Christian traditions increase our awe for God or, to the contrary, weaken our entire faith system because of their patent implausibility? And are our "dark" and their "dark," perhaps, the same?

Miracle stories were supposed to make people living in a prescientific era—a world of superstition and mystery—more faithful, more in awe of God. And while there is a tendency today to make fun of devout Catholics or Southern Baptists who frequent shrines or faith healers in search of miraculous cures, it was an eighteenth-century Hassidic rabbi, Mendel of Rymanov, who said, "If a thousand believing Hasidim were to gather around a block of wood, it would perform miracles"—their "dark" and our "dark." Even today, it is futile to try to argue demographics or morality with a religio-nationalistic settler in the "West Bank" area of Israel. Explain to him that the Arab population in that area will inevitably overwhelm the Jewish population and he will raise his eyes to heaven and respond, "*Yisrael, b'tah baAdonai* (Israel, trust in God!)" If Sarah could have a child in her nineties, if hundreds of thousands could gorge on quail in the wilderness, if Elijah could ascend to the heavens in a chariot, if Elisha could bring back the dead and perform a score of other wonders—all displays of the power of God—why bother me with rationalism?

Permit me a shocking non sequitur: I do not believe that any of the suspensions of natural law that are recorded in the Bible actually happened, yet I believe that they are true. Again?! I do not believe that any of the suspensions of natural law that are recorded in the Bible actually happened, yet I believe that they are true. The rationalist will have no problem with the first half of that formulation, but what of the second? Let me put it another way.

When the story of an event has been told and retold and retold again for a hundred generations, then that event is true, whether it actually happened or not! So many traditions and prayers and ceremonies have been created along the way since the original telling, so many principles of faith have been connected to that event/nonevent since it was first related around a tribal campfire, that it really does not matter whether or not it did, in fact, happen. Here are some examples:

— I believe/do not believe that God revealed the Ten Commandments to Israel at Mount Sinai. Whether or not there was an actual miraculous revelation at Sinai, the commandments and subsequently, the Torah are the foundations of Western civilization. I have no doubt that the Torah is the product of several God-inspired priests, prophets, and scribes who lived and wrote over a period of several hundred years; but at least since the days of Ezra (fifth century BCE) the people of Israel has had that

Torah and has treated it, taught it, and lived it as if it were literally the revealed word of God at Sinai. And so it is.

— I believe/do not believe that there ever was an Adam or an Eve or a Garden of Eden. But that story is so remarkably prescient in its recognition that while the human being might yearn for the ease, security, and irresponsibility of Eden, to be human is to make often difficult choices, choices that might be good or bad, and that we must then live with the consequences of those choices. To live in Eden is to be a plaything of God, a marionette dancing meaninglessly at the whim of the manipulator; to have been expelled from Eden is to be given the gift of free will, the opportunity to be a cocreator with God. And so, yes—we were born in Eden and then expelled.

— A distinguished colleague in a somewhat traditional congregation made the mistake of mentioning in the course of a Passover sermon that he did not actually believe in the historicity of the ten plagues or that the entire people of Israel participated in the Exodus. That statement precipitated a severe reaction and disapproval from a large part of the congregation. Was he correct? Yes . . . but no. I do not believe that God sent down a series of plagues on the Egyptians and that six hundred thousand adult male Hebrews left Egypt and spent forty years wandering in the Sinai wilderness with Moses. But the celebration of those events by the people of Israel for three millennia and the retelling of that story each and every one of those three thousand years (*Haggadah*) along with the ritual ingestion of matzah, bitter herbs, and wine, has made the Exodus a basic truth of Judaism. God freed the children of Israel from Egypt through signs and wonders (and God freed the black slaves of America who believed that Moses said, "Old Pharaoh, let My people go"). It is true.

One of the great intellectual tragedies of Western history was the rejection of religion by so many of the great eighteenth-century French and British philosophers. The "Age of Reason" produced an utter disdain for sacred scripture and the faith systems that evolved from those scriptures. There is no doubt that a tremendous amount of corruption had tainted the teachings of the church and that such corruption needed to be exposed. But the reaction of the philosophers was extreme, a good example of throwing out the baby with the bathwater. Voltaire's *Dictionnaire Philosophique* was a relentlessly antireligious effort to *"écrasez l'infame"* (to crush infamy); and by infamy, Voltaire meant the irrational teachings and the power of the church.

In his essay "On Miracles," Scottish philosopher David Hume attacked religion generally because of its reliance on miracles:

> There is not to be found, in all history, any miracle attested by a sufficient number of men, of such unquestioned good sense, education, and learning, as to secure us against all delusion in themselves; of such undoubted integrity, as to place them beyond all suspicion of any design to deceive others; . . . and at the same time attesting facts, performed in such a public manner, and in so celebrated a part of the world, as to render the detection unavoidable.

For Hume, as for most of the rationalists of his era, it was necessary to attack and expose religion, not only the miracle-rife Christianity that they grew up with but, by extension, all religion:

> Opposing one species of superstition to another, set them a quarreling; while we ourselves, during their fury and contention, happily make our escape into the calm, though obscure, regions of philosophy. (*The Natural History of Religion*)

Religion has, in modern times, taken a "bad rap" because its basic scriptures are so saturated with the miraculous. Most people do not have the critical faculties to be able to separate the essential from the peripheral. If a religion today teaches miracles as literal truth, then it deserves the opprobrium of philosophers and serious thinkers. If religion is to continue to be an effective force in society, then it must boldly declare its independence from the incredible. A religion is supposed to be a system of truth; it is supposed to provide its adherents with criteria for recognizing falsehood. How can it do so if it persists in adhering to dogmas which require the suspension of reason?

Of course, a religion can go too far in its rejection of the supernatural. I will never forget the time when, in an effort to understand our neighbors better, my congregation invited the children of a nearby Unitarian church to meet with our own children for a discussion on Easter and Passover. It was painful to listen to the Unitarian children attempting to explain Easter. There was a lot of "Jesus was a good man," "Jesus was a great teacher," but there was no resurrection, not even as metaphor, nothing inspiring awe that might make those children want to perpetuate either Easter or Unitarianism. At the other end of the spectrum, of course, are the Roman Catholics and the several mainstream Protestant denominations that still include in their creeds, as essential articles of faith, the virgin birth and the resurrection.

I am bound in kinship to ancestors who believed in the supernatural, who prayed for miracles, and some of whom actually believed that they had witnessed miracles. I am bound in kinship to Sarah and Moses and Elisha, but if I today were to be satisfied with their theology or the theologies of those who told their stories, then I would not deserve to call myself a teacher of Judaism. One of those ancestors to whom I am also bound, Rabbi Hanina bar Hama (third century), taught, "The seal of God is truth." Any element in a religion that cannot stand up to the most rigorous requirements of truth cannot be defended and can only ultimately be destructive of that religion.

What does it mean to truly believe in God? It means to believe that the human being was created with an innate sensitivity to the will of God; some call it "the image of God." It means that there is a purpose to life and that, through study and humility and service, one might even catch a glimpse of God. It means that our task in life is to search every day for a deeper understanding of God. It means that we petty human beings can rise to the state of partnership with God in the fashioning of a nobler world. It means to recognize that every day of our lives is potentially a miracle.

Turn 8

Come over and sit down here,
Ploni Almoni.

—Ruth 4:1

The locution *Ploni Almoni*, which is the Hebrew equivalent of John Doe, appears only three times in the Bible. In two instances, in the books of Samuel and Kings, it occurs quite naturally, in both cases representing an unnamed place, a secret place that is better not divulged. In the book of Ruth, though, it is not at all a natural locution; the speaker, Boaz, certainly knew the name of the man whom he addressed as *Ploni Almoni*. The two of them lived in the same town, Bethlehem; they were, in fact, related; and they were about to participate in a ceremony in the presence of "*ten elders of the town*" who also knew both men. And so why did Boaz not call to him by his actual name? Or we might ask more properly, Why did the author of Ruth refuse to record the name of the person summoned by Boaz, substituting for it *Ploni Almoni*?

This question is not inconsequential. In the entire brief book of Ruth, there are only seven named characters, and each of those seven was given a name that tells the reader something about his or her personality or fate. Clearly, the reader should not take Ruth to be history. It is a novella, probably written around the eighth century BCE by a talented author whose primary purpose was to establish a romantic genealogy for King David. And so the names recorded in the book are not the names of actual historic personalities but rather names given by the author to tell us something about his dramatis personae. (There are some Bible critics who place the authorship several centuries later and read it as a polemic against the strictures forbidding foreign marriages in the books of Ezra and Nehemiah. My own inclination is toward the earlier dating, but in either case the problem of the locution *Ploni Almoni* remains.)

There is at least one other instance in the Bible of a name chosen to alert the reader to the character of its bearer. In 1 Samuel 25, we read about the boorishness of a wealthy Carmelite by the name of Nabal. That Nabal's name is not incidental to the story of the meeting of David and Abigail is implicit in the repetition of his name eighteen times within just thirty-six verses of the chapter. One of those verses, though, is very explicit: Abigail, begging for mercy from the hot-headed young David, says, "*Please, my Lord, pay no attention to this wretched fellow, Nabal. For he is just as his name says: his name means 'boor' and he is a boor*" (25:25). We might say the same for seven of the eight characters in the story of Ruth; they are just as their names imply.

The author of Ruth may have been among the first who used the foreshadowing device of suggestive naming, but he certainly was not the last. I offer two notable examples from English literature, Shakespeare and Dickens. A brief sampling from Shakespeare: Aguecheek, Froth, Pinch, Pistol, and of course, Sir Toby Belch. And from Dickens: Pecksniff, Bumble, Vholes, Verisopht, and Jellyby. Back, now, to Ruth and the problem of *Ploni Almoni*.

I am by no means the first student of Bible to recognize the significance of the names in Ruth. Virtually all the commentators, going back to the rabbis of the Talmud, offered interpretations. The Talmud suggests that two of the characters, Mahlon and Chilion, actually had other given names, Joash and Seraph (the names of two men who, like Mahlon and Chilion, "*married into Moab*," as recorded in a genealogy in 1 Chronicles 4), and that their names were changed by the author of Ruth in order to give the reader some information about them:

> They were called Mahlon and Chilion [for this reason]: Mahlon, because they profaned their bodies, and Chilion, because they were condemned by the Omnipresent to destruction. (*Baba Bathra* 91b)

Whether or not we accept the etymologies offered by the Talmudic sages, it is clear that these names were meant to alert the reader to something about the characters of Mahlon and Chilion. The same is true of all the other personae of Ruth—Elimelech, Naomi, Ruth, Orpah, and Boaz, with the exception of Mr. John Doe, *Ploni Almoni*. And it is worthy of note that there are no other characters in the entire Bible who bear these seven names. (*Chilion*, as a word meaning "destruction," does occur twice and *Boaz* occurs, along with *Jachin*, as one of the two pillars of Solomon's Temple.)

The book of Ruth opens by introducing us to six characters:

A man of Bethlehem in Judah, with his wife and two sons, went to reside in the country of Moab. The man's name was Elimelech, his wife's name was Naomi, and his two sons were named Mahlon and Chilion . . . Elimelech, Naomi's husband, died, and she was left with her two sons. They married Moabite women, one named Orphah and the other Ruth. (1:1-4)

— Elimelech is a name that denotes nobility—*Eli* (my God) and *melech* (king). He was a prominent landowner in Bethlehem, related to other landowners, and there is the rabbinic suggestion that his pride and his willingness to leave the land of Israel brought about his death.

— Naomi derives from the Hebrew root *noam*, meaning "sweet" or "pleasant." Another hint about the significance of the names in Ruth occurs at the end of the first chapter where Naomi chides the people who greet her by name on her return to Bethlehem by saying, "*Call me not Naomi* [meaning pleasant]; *call me Mara* [meaning bitter], *for the Almighty has made my lot very bitter.*"

— Mahlon derives from the Hebrew root *holeh*, meaning "sick." There is the suggestion (in the Talmudic passage above) that it derives from *halal*, meaning "profanation." In either case this name, like the next, clearly connotes something bad for which one might be punished by early death.

— Chilion derives from the Hebrew root *calah* meaning "destruction" or "termination," again suggesting something bad.

— Ruth is a name that presents a bit of a problem in that it does not obviously derive from any Hebrew root. Most commentators, though, read it as a contraction of *reut*, meaning "love" or "friendship." (It is interesting, but probably not relevant, to note that there is an English word *ruth*, derived from Middle English, that means "compassion," the opposite of ruthless.) The fact that all the other names have obvious connotations makes it more than likely that this name would have been recognized in the biblical period as meaning something like love or friendship. Ruth's actions, of course, bear this out.

— Orpah derives from the Hebrew root *oref* meaning "the back of the neck." Most commentators suggest (Midrash *Ruth Rabbah 2, Yalkut Shimoni*

Ruth) that this name reminds us that, whereas Ruth remained with her mother-in-law, Naomi, Orpah finally turned her back on her and *"returned to her people and her gods."*

— Boaz does not appear until chapter 2, but he is immediately introduced as a *gibbor hayil*, a mighty man or a man of substance, one to be reckoned with and taken seriously. The name derives from the root *oz*, meaning "strength." *Bo-az* might mean "in him there is strength." As indicated above, the name Boaz also occurs in the book of 1 Kings as the name of one of the two great columns that supported the portico of the temple of Solomon, Jachin and Boaz. This too would suggest strength.

Now that we have seen that all of the names in the book of Ruth reveal something about the characters themselves, let's proceed to a brief recap of the familiar story and to the character who is introduced only as *Ploni Almoni*, John Doe. One can read through the entire book in under half an hour and the charming little story is certainly well worth the effort, but here it is in capsule:

> Because of a famine in Judah, Elimelech, Naomi, and their two sons, Malhlon and Chilion, migrated to Moab. The two sons married Moabite women, Ruth and Orpah, and then the father and the two sons died. Naomi decided to return to her former home in Bethlehem, and her daughters-in-law wanted to go with her. She succeeded in dissuading Orpah, but Ruth insisted, vowing famously, *"Wherever you go, I will go; . . . your people shall be my people, and your God my God."*

> Arriving penniless in Bethlehem at the beginning of the grain harvest, Ruth went to glean in the field of Boaz, a kinsman of Elimelech, who was very kind to her. Naomi saw the possibility of a levirate marriage (see Deut. 25:5-10) for Ruth, and advised Ruth to seek Boaz's protection. Boaz determined to take responsibility for Ruth, but first he had to arrange for a closer kinsman, the one referred to as *Ploni Almoni*, to renounce his claim on Ruth. Boaz and Ruth then married, and the son whom they produced, Obed, was the grandfather of King David.

And so the question: Why did the author choose to call the closer kinsman *Ploni Almoni* rather than by his proper name, whatever that might have been? As the fourth and final chapter of Ruth opens, Boaz goes to the city gate, the place where judgment was rendered and business was conducted, and he waited until the closer kinsman passed by.

> *He called, "Come over and sit down here, Ploni Almoni." And he came over and sat down. Then [Boaz] took ten elders of the town and said, "Be seated here," and they sat down. He said to the redeemer, "Naomi, now returned from the country of Moab, must sell the piece of land which belonged to our kinsman Elimelech. I thought I should disclose the matter to you and say: 'Acquire it in the presence of those seated here and in the presence of the elders of the people.' If you are willing to redeem it, redeem. But if you will not redeem it, tell me that I may know. For there is no one to redeem but you, and I come after you.*

The anonymous kinsman, realizing that he can acquire some good real estate at a distress sale price, immediately answers affirmatively. But then Boaz goes on to drop the bomb:

> *When you acquire the property from Naomi and from Ruth the Moabite, you must also acquire the wife of the deceased so as to perpetuate the name of the deceased upon his estate.*

Notice that in his opening salvo, Boaz says nothing about Ruth or marriage. The prospect of acquiring unencumbered property has John Doe salivating. Then, having established the fact that Mr. Doe would be happy to profit from the misfortune of Naomi, Boaz goes on to the matter of responsibility for the Moabite widow, Ruth. A levirate marriage and the subsequent birth of a son who would be, in effect, the son of Mahlon meant that a part of Mr. Doe's estate would then belong to that new son. That is the essence of the levirate law, i.e., "*to perpetuate the name of the deceased.*" That prospect does not at all appeal to Mr. Doe who demurs, "*Lest I impair my own estate.*"

We are dealing here with a greedy, venal character who clearly has no interest in the welfare of two widows or in the perpetuation of somebody else's name.

He sloughs off any responsibility, saying to Boaz, "*Acquire for yourself,*" and he then goes through the prescribed ceremony for the renunciation of responsibility. He then disappears from the story while Boaz remains with the elders and assumes responsibility for the two women "*so as to perpetuate the name of the deceased upon his estate.*"

Three times in that scene by the city gate we hear repeated the refrain "*to perpetuate the name*" or "*that the name of the deceased may not disappear.*" And then, after the legalities are completed, how do the elders react? They bless Boaz for his kindness, asking God to "*perpetuate your [i.e., Boaz's] name in Bethlehem.*" And, as if to fulfill that blessing, the very next verse informs us of the marriage of Ruth and Boaz and of the birth of their son. And how do the women of Bethlehem react to all of this good fortune? They too bless Boaz, exclaiming, "*May his name be perpetuated in Israel!*"

With all of this name perpetuating, whose name, by contrast, is *not* perpetuated? Of course, the closer kinsman, Mr. Anonymous, John Doe, *Ploni Almoni.* His name has disappeared. The author, of course, could have simply referred to him throughout as the redeemer or as the nearest kinsman. Or he might have invented a name for him, as he did with the seven other characters in the story, a name like *Ichabod* (without honor) or *Ish-boshet* (man of shame). But to make it crystal clear that he was contrasting the *absence* of this man's name with the *perpetuation* of the names of Mahlon and, of course, of the hero, Boaz, he is labeled *Ploni Almoni,* the nameless one, the one whose name has been erased from the annals of his people.

One of the worst curses that one can utter against a despicable person goes back to biblical days. After the incident of the golden calf, God threatens to wipe out the entire people of Israel: "*I will destroy them and blot out their name from under heaven*" (Deut. 9:14). What is the punishment prescribed for those who abandon God and worship idols? "*Adonai blots out his name from under heaven*" (Deut. 29:19). The psalmist invoked God's curse against his enemies: "*May their names be blotted out!*" (Ps. 109:13). That curse persists to modern times. As a child, I thought that Hitler's last name was *Yimah shmo* because any time that his name was mentioned by my parents, it was followed in the same breath by *Yimah shmo,* which I later learned meant "may his name be blotted out."

I believe that the author of Ruth was indicating to his readers in the most dramatic fashion the punishment that God metes out to those who refuse to take responsibility for the welfare of their kin. Their names will be blotted out. What was the fate of Boaz who graciously took it upon himself to support Naomi and Ruth and to perpetuate the name of the deceased Mahlon? His name was perpetuated. What was the fate of the failed redeemer, the one who had the opportunity to exemplify nobility and humanity but sloughed it off in order to preserve his wealth? His name was blotted out. In a book that makes an emphatic point with each and every name recorded, his name is *not* recorded. He is John Doe, *Ploni Almoni*.

Turn 9

You shall not boil a kid in its mother's milk.

—Exodus 23:19, 34:26 and
Deuteronomy 14:21

Kashrut, the system of Jewish dietary regulations, has long been the single most recognizable aspect of Jewish behavior. There were eras in Jewish history when Jews were persecuted and even executed because they adhered to certain features of kashrut, most notably the avoidance of pork products. But even today in the open societies of the Western democracies, where Jews often choose not to observe kashrut, virtually everyone, Jew and non-Jew alike, is familiar with at least two main features of the historic Jewish dietary regimen, i.e., the avoidance of pork products and the separation of milk and meat.

Kashrut is so ancient and so conspicuous a part of Judaism that it cannot be ignored, even by Jews who are repelled by what they consider to be a system of taboos and superstitions which, reverting to the language of Reform's Pittsburgh Platform of 1885, are "altogether foreign to our present mental and spiritual state." It is, of course, an essential part of Orthodox and Conservative Judaism, and recent statements of the more liberal Jewish denominations in North America have recommended at least some degree of adherence to kashrut. Before we go on to comment on the validity, or nonvalidity, of kashrut for Jews today, it would be instructive to review those dietary laws that survive from antiquity and then proceed to the question of their importance, if at all, for modern Jews.

Possibly the best known of all the dietary laws is the very cryptic: "*You shall not boil a kid in its mother's milk,*" which I have chosen as the supertext for this essay. This injunction was interpreted by later generations of Jewish authorities to forbid the eating or preparing of dairy products and meat together. Whether or not that was the original intent is open to question, as we shall see below, but whatever its interpretation, it is an essential pillar of the structure of kashrut.

Almost equally familiar is the prohibition against the eating of animals that do not have cloven hooves and do not chew their cud (i.e., ruminants) in Leviticus 11:3. This injunction allows for the eating of most domestic animals, e.g., cattle, sheep, goats, and deer, with the notable exceptions of pigs, horses, camels, and donkeys. The same chapter in Leviticus lists twenty birds (one of them actually a rodent) or species of birds that are prohibited. The chapter also enumerates those insects which may or may not be eaten.

Somewhat less familiar to most people and curiously, less observed today is the prohibition against all sea creatures that do not have scales and fins (Lev. 11:9). Although this prohibition is no less prominent than the ones above, it is not unusual to find Jews who avoid nonkosher animals and who do not mix milk and meat but who yet partake of such shellfish as lobster and shrimp.

Even less familiar to most people are the prohibitions against the eating of animal fat and blood (Lev. 3:17, 7:23) and the prohibition against the eating of any animal that has died of natural causes or that was "torn by beasts" (Lev. 22:8 and Exod. 22:30). The term used by the Torah to indicate "torn by beasts" is *t'reifah,* and somehow over the centuries that word was expanded by popular usage to include all nonkosher food. For most Jews, whether or not they are familiar with the prescriptions of kashrut, food is either kosher or *treif.*

Having now reviewed the basic laws of kashrut, I pose four questions.

First, should the eating habits of Jews today be delimited by a set of laws and taboos that originated in the sacred texts of a prescientific society?

Second, should the eating habits of reasonable people be determined by any considerations beyond health?

Third, shall we cede to medieval sages and to those who claim to be their successors today the right to determine how a cryptic ancient text should be interpreted?

And finally, shall we also cede to these sages the right to determine what constitutes the humane treatment of animals?

The first of those four questions is clearly the most essential, for if one believes that the Torah in its entirety was written or dictated by God, then no human being has the right to dispute even one letter of it. If, on the other hand, one believes that the Torah and the subsequent prophetic and early rabbinic writings were the products of God-inspired but fallible human beings, then one has the right and even the obligation to examine those writings and to subject them to critical analysis. This essay is intended for readers who reverently think of God as the creative spirit of the universe and who equally reverently think of human beings as endowed by God with the intelligence and critical faculties to differentiate between what is sacred and timeless and what may be the product of human beings who, however well-intentioned, were influenced by the mores, rites, and taboos of their times.

I believe that we have every right to reconsider the laws of kashrut and to determine, with due respect for history and tradition, which of those laws should be determinative for us today. But I believe equally that every sensitive human being, Jew or non-Jew, should evolve a personal dietary regimen which accords with the basic meaning of the word *kasher* (or kosher), i.e., fitting and proper. Although my personal eating habits would not be considered kosher by those who see themselves as the guardians of *halakha* (traditional rabbinic law) today, I would argue that those habits are very much in keeping with the spirit and intent of the Torah.

And so to the second question: should our eating habits be determined by any considerations beyond health? I respond with an emphatic yes. In eating, as in every other human activity, there are ethical questions that must be considered. Should food be considered kosher if its production involves pain to animals or the despoliation of natural resources? If it is eaten without any indication of gratitude? If it is not shared by other human beings or animals?

There are those who consider the eating of any animal, fish, or fowl to be unethical because it involves the killing of living creatures. I have no argument with vegetarians and vegans. Possibly, they have achieved a level of ethical behavior that is beyond me and, I believe, beyond the capabilities of most people and certainly beyond the ethics of biblical tradition. I consider vegetarianism to be a form of kashrut, but this essay is directed primarily to the vast majority of people who do eat meat and/or fish and fowl.

While I do not myself eat mammal flesh, I am not ready to condemn those who do. But I firmly believe that those who do eat such meat are obliged by consideration of ethics to see to it that whatever they eat has been produced with the least possible pain to animals. It should not be necessary to describe the cruel methods that are employed to produce, for example, paté de foie gras and "milk-fed" veal; the distress of force-fed geese and immobilized calves have been widely reported. One of the great ethical teachings of Judaism is *tzaar baalei hayim* (relieving the pain of animals). There is no shortage of verses in the Torah that require sensitivity to the feelings of animals. A few examples should suffice.

> *You shall not muzzle an ox while it is threshing.* (Deut. 25:4)

> *When an ox or a sheep or a goat is born, it shall remain with its mother for seven days, and on the eighth day it is acceptable as an offering . . . No animal from the herd or from the flock shall be slaughtered on the same day with its young.* (Lev. 22:27-28)

> *If . . . you happen upon a bird's nest, . . . with fledglings or eggs and the mother sitting over the fledglings or the eggs, do not take the mother together with her young. Let the mother go and take only the young in order that you may fare well and have a long life.* (Deut. 22:6-7)

> *If you see your enemy's animal lying under its burden and would refrain from raising it, you must nevertheless raise it with him.* (Exod. 23:5)

While there is no law in the Torah that states specifically that one must treat animals humanely, it was quite clear to the sages of the Talmud that this was the intent of the passages above. "Relieving the pain of animals (*tzaar baalei hayim*)," they ruled, "is commanded by the Torah" (i.e., it supercedes rabbinic law) (*Baba Metzia* 32b and *Shabbat* 128b).

Certainly, personal health should always be a major factor in determining one's eating habits, but the pain that one might cause to other living creatures by choosing to eat this or that food must also be taken into serious consideration by any ethical person. Furthermore, I believe that it is gluttonous to eat any food without at least pausing to acknowledge the source of that food. For some, this will mean a prayer of thanks to God before breaking bread while for others it might mean a simple moment of reflection. We should remind ourselves each time that we participate in this most bestial act of eating that we are, in fact, not beasts.

In this regard, I will always remember a lesson that my father taught me as a young boy. We were studying the passage in Genesis that tells of how Esau sold his birthright to his brother Jacob for a bowl of lentil stew. The text reads, *"[Esau] ate and drank and rose and left. Thus did Esau spurn the birthright."* (Gen. 25:34) In what way, my father asked, did Esau demonstrate that he despised the sacred birthright? In that he ate and drank and rose and left, without taking even a moment to thank God for his food. From that day to this, I have never been able to eat a meal without at least pausing to consider the source of my nourishment.

And of course, a further proof of our humanity in the act of eating is our resolve to provide food for those who are not as fortunate as we might be. Every moral human being must either give food directly to needy people or contribute regularly to organizations that provide food for the hungry and homeless. And a related consideration must be a proper regard for the toil and the rights of those laborers who participate in the harvesting and production of our food. Examples of the exploitation of seasonal farm workers are numerous and notorious. One should carefully avoid buying foods that are seasoned by the sweat of exploited workers. These two elements must also be features of any ethical system of kashrut.

And there is yet another consideration beyond health in our determination of what foods we should or should not eat. I alluded above to periods of persecution when Jews were either forced to eat pig flesh or executed because of their refusal to do so. One of the features of the Hellenistic persecution of Jews that led to the Maccabean revolt was the insistence of King Antiochus IV that Jews eat pig flesh and offer pigs on the altar of the temple. In Spain and Portugal after the fifteenth- and sixteenth-century expulsions, one method used by agents of the Inquisition to ferret out crypto-Jews was their avoidance of pork. Inquisitorial records tell of crypto-Jews who would keep pots of pig meat boiling outside their homes in order to mislead the inquisitors, but somehow, many of those Jews could not bring themselves, even at the risk of arrest, to eat it. It is very likely that it is this historic memory, rather than the Torah text that equally forbids shrimp and rabbits, that keeps a large proportion of the modern Jewish community from eating pork.

As to our third question, re the interpretation of a cryptic text from the Torah, we now come to that well-known verse on which the rabbis of old based the prohibition on the eating meat and dairy products together: *"You shall not boil a kid in its mother's milk."* I would contend that this very familiar law has absolutely nothing to do with the mixing of milk and meat but that it is another of those injunctions that were intended to teach *tzaar baalei hayim*. This matter has been widely argued over the centuries, but I believe that the most telling proof that this law has nothing to do with the dietary prohibitions is the fact that it does not appear in the exhaustive list of dietary laws specified in Leviticus 11.

"You shall not boil a kid in its mother's milk" appears three times in the Torah. In two instances, it occurs at the conclusion of passages that have to do with festival sacrifices (Exod. 23 and 34). In the third instance, which does indeed deal with dietary laws, (Deut. 14), it is appended to the concluding admonition, *"You are a people consecrated to the Lord your God"* and it is clearly disconnected from the dietary laws that precede it. I agree with the opinion of the twelfth-century biblical commentator, Rashbam (Rabbi Samuel ben Meir), that "it is disgraceful and voracious and gluttonous to consume the mother's milk together with its young. This law is comparable to *Leviticus 22:28* and *Deuteronomy* 22:6-7 [see above]. The Torah gave this commandment in order to teach you how to behave in a civilized manner." Maimonides, in his *Guide for the Perplexed*, suggested that one of the reasons for this prohibition is "because it is somehow connected with idolatry" (*Guide* 3, 48). It is as if the Torah were teaching us: "You, Israel, are consecrated to God, therefore you must not behave in the abominably insensitive manner of your neighbors who do, in fact, boil a kid in its mother's milk."

I feel certain that my readers will never boil a kid in its mother's milk, not because that law has anything to do with the mixing of milk and meat but because to do so would be as callous as killing a mother bird together with its babies or muzzling a working animal. These are all ethical dicta and have absolutely nothing to do with drinking milk or eating cheese along with meat or fowl. Yet what mountains of sophistry have been balanced by the medieval rabbis on the horns of that one hapless kid (reminiscent of the poor *Had Gadya* of the Passover Seder)! A facetious dialogue between God and Moses that was making the rounds a few years ago is instructive:

> God: Moses, tell the people that they must not boil a kid in its mother's milk.

> Moses: Yes, Lord, I will instruct the people as you command. (*He goes and delivers God's word to the multitude. A few days go by, and then he returns.*)

Moses:	O Lord, the people want to know whether they can eat milk and meat together.
God:	Moses, I said, *"You shall not boil a kid in its mother's milk."*
Moses:	Yes, Lord, I understand. But they also want to know if they have to have two sets of dishes.
God:	Moses, I said, *"You shall not boil a kid in its mother's milk."*
Moses:	Yes, Lord, I hear You. But the people want to know if they have to wait six hours after meat before they can drink a glass of milk.
God:	Moses (*rather impatiently*), I said, *"You shall not boil a kid in its mother's milk!"*
Moses:	Yes, I understand, O long-suffering and patient Lord. But the people want to know if they must bury a dairy spoon in the earth for a few days if it accidentally touches meat.
God:	MOSES (*the mountain begins to quake*), I SAID, *"YOU SHALL NOT BOIL A KID IN ITS MOTHER'S MILK!!"*
Moses:	Yes, God of Mercy, I understand. But the people want to know if they can wash their dairy and meat dishes in the same sink.
God:	I'm out of here! Tell the people to do whatever the @>#^% they want!!!

If one chooses to keep milk and meat separate, recognizing the common practice of Jewish communities for two millennia, I can certainly understand and even honor that choice. But I cannot entertain the notion that the admonition not to boil a kid in its mother's milk has anything at all to do with the mixing of milk and meat. It is purely and simply a law intended to encourage civilized behavior.

Proceeding to the fourth and final question, about the humane treatment of animals, we must address the issue of *shehitah* (ritual slaughter) as it is practiced today. The fact that both the U. S. Department of Agriculture and the organization People for the Ethical Treatment of Animals have raised questions about the humaneness of kosher slaughter (particularly in the notorious slaughtering plant in Postville, Iowa, described in the book *Postville* by Stephen G. Bloom, 2000) should be an embarrassment to the Orthodox kashrut authorities who give their approval to such slaughter.

These same Orthodox authorities certify the kashrut of butcher shops that sell foie gras and "milk-fed" veal with no consideration whatsoever of the pain of the animals involved. It should be an embarrassment not only to the Orthodox authorities but to all who buy kosher meat that the U.S. Humane Slaughtering Act of 1978, which requires the stunning of animals before they are killed so as to avoid unnecessary pain and the sensing of impending slaughter, must make an exception for *shehitah*.

The laws of *shehitah* require that an animal be killed as swiftly and painlessly as possible. But according to an expose in the *New York Times* (March 10, 2006), in the Iowa slaughtering plant operated by Agriprocessors, the largest producer of meat certified by Orthodox authorities as *glatt* (see below) kosher, in certain instances, "A second worker would step in after the first cut by the *shochet*, or ritual slaughterer. He would use a knife to open the animal's neck further and reach in with a hook to pull out the trachea and esophagus, with the carotid arteries attached. This was done to speed bleeding; kosher meat must contain as little blood as possible." Further in the article, a supervisor at the plant conceded that the trachea-pulling "should not occur while an animal is conscious or sensory." So much for the Orthodox authorities, bound by the strictures of the sixteenth-century *Shulhan Arukh* (*Code of Jewish Law*), with little or no consideration for what must be the cornerstone of any system of kashrut, the sacred principle of *tzaar baalei hayim*.

Just a few words about that anomaly that is generally referred to as *glatt kosher*. There was a much less contentious period within the American Jewish community, generally before the 1970s, when Orthodox rabbis were quite comfortable sitting with Reform and Conservative rabbis and when there was hardly any awareness of the term *glatt*, which simply means "smooth" in Yiddish. According to the laws of *shehitah* which may be found in *Yoreh Deah*, chapters 1-28 (the section of the *Shulhan Arukh* that deals with the dietary laws), the lungs of a kosher animal must be examined to be sure that they are smooth, i.e., free of adhesions. But there are various types of adhesions that may be found in the lungs of animals, some of which are minor and do not render the animal unkosher. However, those who impose more rigid standards of kashrut on themselves will insist on eating only those animals whose lungs are absolutely smooth, i.e., *glatt*.

There is a growing and, I believe, unhealthy tendency within Orthodoxy to take on more and more restrictions as indications of greater piety. It is this tendency which has led to the ubiquity of *glatt kosher* butcher shops, restaurants, and groceries since the 1980s. That this tendency can lead to ridiculous extremes is attested to by the existence today of dairy or vegetarian restaurants and of packaged nonmeat foods that present themselves as *glatt*, a term which should only be applied to the lungs of animals. The term *glatt kosher* has taken on the connotation of superkosher and Orthodox supervisory authorities seem not to disapprove of this distinction.

My personal attitude toward *glatt kosher* can be summarized by an incident in an El Al plane back in 1995. I was traveling to Israel with a delegation of Philadelphia Jewish leaders to attend the thirty-day memorial for Israeli Prime Minister Yitzhak Rabin. When the time came for dinner, a flight attendant came to me and a few others before the general service with specially wrapped meals. I asked her why I was being served before my traveling companions, and she answered that my meal was a special *glatt kosher* one. I told her that I could not accept a so-called *glatt* dinner because I considered it to be *treif*. She shrugged and took it away, but my companions asked me what I meant by my characterization of *glatt kosher* as *treif*.

I explained to them that food is either kosher or nonkosher and that the food served by El Al Airlines was kosher. I explained further that any food which is represented as superkosher could only discourage people from eating what is normally accepted as kosher because it would seem to be of inferior kashrut. Bad enough that kosher food companies charge much higher prices for their products, but then to cast doubt on already overpriced kosher foods by touting a higher variety of kashrut is both ridiculous and unethical.

This comparatively recent phenomenon of *glatt kosher* food is yet another condemnation of those rabbinic authorities who have made a lucrative business of kashrut. One has every right—ethically, historically, or spiritually—to decide to observe a dietary regimen in keeping with Jewish tradition. But to cede the right to decide which foods one may eat to rabbinic authorities who ignore critical scholarship, who are bound by the narrowest interpretations of medieval pietists, who often ignore the principle of *tzaar baalei hayim*, and who are all too often influenced by the contributions of businessmen who profit from the vagaries of kashrut supervision is certainly not to observe what is best and noblest in Jewish tradition.

I believe in kashrut, and I heartily recommend it to all who want to participate in the richness and the blessings of Jewish tradition. I consider our family dining table to be a *mizbeah me-at*, a miniature or a proxy altar. On the Sabbath and festivals, our table is graced by wine, candles, and *hallot*; it is a sacred space which connects us to God and to the history of our people. Even on ordinary days, one's table should represent something more than catering to our basest animal instinct: eating.

But the kashrut that I recommend and that I observe is not the kashrut of the Orthodox Union. It is a dietary regimen that derives from an enlightened understanding of the ancient admonition: *"You shall not boil a kid in its mother's milk,"* and its primary requirements are

- sensitivity to the pain of animals,
- acts of tzedakah to the hungry,
- expressions of gratitude for sustenance,
- the avoidance of gluttony,
- consideration of the food taboos of previous generations,
- the avoidance of foods that are reminiscent of historic persecutions, and
- the avoidance of foods that are the produced through the exploitation of laborers.

This is kashrut, choosing to eat only that which is fitting and proper for an observant ethical Jew.

Turn 10

*Can a woman forget her baby,
or abandon the child
of her womb?*

—Isaiah 49:15

"Isaiah is to be considered the work of two distinct authors: First Isaiah (chs. 1-39) whose prophetic career in Jerusalem covers the years c. 740-700 B.C.E., and that of an unknown prophet (Deutero-Isaiah, chs. 40-66) whose prophecies reflect the experience and events of the Babylonian Exile c. 540 B.C.E." (*Encyclopedia Judaica,* vol. 9, p. 46)

I would add to that succinct explanation the possibility that the material in chapters 40-66, plus some few fragments from the earlier chapters, might be the products of more than one unknown prophet. Whereas First Isaiah castigated the people for failing to live up to their covenant with God and predicted severe punishment, Deutero-Isaiah (i.e., the anonymous prophet or prophets), prophesying after the calamitous destruction of Judah, was the Comforter of Israel, explaining that Adonai is universal and has used the Babylonians as the rod of His anger. But now that Israel has been punished for all her sins, God instructs the prophet: *"Speak tenderly to Jerusalem, and declare to her that her term of service is over, that her iniquity is expiated, for she has received at the hand of Adonai double for all her sins."*

We shall refer to the author(s) of chapters 40-66 as D-Isaiah, as distinct from the Isaiah of the eighth century BCE.

* * *

Imagine a gathering of refugees in some village on the Euphrates or a parallel gathering of bereaved survivors, camped outside a demolished Judaean city, keening hopelessly, not knowing where to turn. To Adonai? But no, Adonai was defeated by the gods of Babylonia, his temple left a smoldering ruin. Never again will priests offer daily sacrifices on Mount Zion; never again will the courtyard of Solomon's Temple be filled with masses of worshipers on the pilgrim festivals, inhaling the "sweet savor" of roasting lambs; never again will Levites stand on the steps of that sacred place singing "*Hallelujah, praise be to Adonai.*" To whom? Adonai is no more! Adonai was consumed in the flames kindled by the cruel worshipers of Marduk. Marduk is all-powerful; he has conquered Adonai. It would be prudent now to turn to Marduk, the god of Nebuchadnezzar.

In the midst of the mourners, though, is a man who has learned a very different lesson from the destruction; a man who took seriously the pronouncements of those earlier prophets who were certain that Adonai would one day punish the people who had accepted the Torah at Sinai and then ignored its laws. They had been warned and warned again by Isaiah, by Micah, and within the memories of some of them, by Jeremiah.

> *Adonai said to me: "Proclaim all these things through the towns of Judah and the streets of Jerusalem. Hear the terms of the covenant and perform them. For I have repeatedly and persistently warned your fathers from the time I brought them out of Egypt to this day, saying: Obey My commands. But they would not listen or give ear; they all followed the willfulness of their evil hearts. So I have brought upon them all the terms of this covenant, because they did not do what I commanded them to do."*
>
> *Assuredly, thus said Adonai: "I am going to bring upon them disaster from which they will not be able to escape. Then they will cry out to me, but I will not listen to them."* (Jer. 11:6-8, 11)

And so this man rose up and spoke. He reminded the people of the words of the preexilic prophets, of their dire warnings that if the people of Judah persisted in their perversion of the terms of the covenant, they would be severely punished. The destruction of Jerusalem and the misery that followed in its wake were inevitable. Your present condition, he explained patiently to the people, does not mean that our God was defeated. No, quite the contrary! It means that Adonai is a God of truth whose prophets are prophets of truth. Adonai predicted destruction if your parents and grandparents failed to live up to the divine requirements of justice and mercy spelled out so clearly in the Torah, and inexorably, destruction has resulted.

But what about the awesome power of Nebuchadnezzar and his army, the minions of Marduk? "Ah," this anonymous prophet replied. "Precisely! Adonai used the great Nebuchadnezzar as the rod of punishment." And he reminded them of the words of the early prophet Isaiah who referred to the hordes of Assyrians who terrorized Judah a century earlier:

> *Ho, Assyria, rod of My anger, in whose hand, as a staff, is My fury!*
> *I send him against an ungodly nation;*
> *I charge him against a people that provokes Me,*
> *to take its spoil and to seize its booty,*
> *and to make it a thing trampled like the mire of the streets.* (Isa. 10:5-6)

"Try to understand," the prophet admonished them. "Can't you see it? Adonai used Nebuchadnezzar; all the kings of flesh and blood are like putty in the hands of the one God. Until now, you thought of Adonai as the God of Israel, just as Marduk was the god of the Babylonians and Baal the god of the Canaanites. But no! Adonai is so powerful that He can use those gods and the kings who serve them at will, as the rod of punishment."

> *The nations are but a drop in a bucket, . . .*
> *All nations are as naught in His sight;*
> *He accounts them as less than nothing . . .*
>
> *He brings potentates to naught,*
> *makes rulers of the earth as nothing . . .*
>
> *If only you would listen to this,*
> *attend and give heed from now on!*
> *Who was it gave Jacob over to despoilment*
> *and Israel to plunderers?*
> *Surely, Adonai against whom they sinned*
> *in whose ways they would not walk*
> *and whose Torah they would not obey.*
> *So He poured out wrath upon them*
> *His anger and the fury of war.* (Isa. 40:15-17, 23; 42:23-25)

Traditional thinking in the wake of the tragedies of years 587-86 had it that Adonai had been defeated and that the people who had worshiped Adonai would have to direct their loyalties elsewhere. D-Isaiah assured them that not only was Adonai still alive, Adonai was omnipotent, directing the destinies of nations and kings. But if that is true, the members of that decimated remnant living among the ruins of Judah cried, what good does that do us in the pitiful circumstances that are ours? Clearly, Adonai has turned away from us, Adonai has forgotten us.

And then D-Isaiah spoke again in the name of God. I can see tears running down his cheeks as he contemplates this ragged, emaciated remnant who were brought up on stories of the glory days of David and Solomon. He can hardly be heard, his voice choked with sobs. It is more a crooning lullaby than a prophetic pronouncement. His body swaying back and forth, his hands over his eyes, he whispers,

> *Zion says: "Adonai has forsaken me, Adonai has forgotten me." Can a woman forget her baby, or abandon the child of her womb? Though she might forget, I will never forget you. See, I have engraved you on the palms of My hands; your walls are ever before Me.*

The people stop their keening; they strain to hear him. What? What did he say? A woman forget her baby? A mother abandon the infant suckling at her breast? Yes, the prophet repeats, *"She might forget, but I will never forget you."* While the Babylonians were destroying the walls of Jerusalem, while they were setting fire to the temple of Solomon, while they were leading your families into exile and goading them to sing songs of Zion, *"I engraved you on the palms of My hands."* Forget My people Israel? The people who I covenanted with at Sinai? Even if your sinfulness tempted Me to forget you, I could not, not even for an instant—*"Your walls are ever before Me."*

Where in all of human literature is there as poignant a cry as this? D-Isaiah was desperately attempting to rekindle the dying spirit of his people. They were convinced that their God was either dead or that He had abandoned them. "No!" the prophet cried. "It is more likely that a mother would abandon her child than that God would abandon you. Such a thing is unimaginable. Remember; Adonai married our people at Sinai. Our God loves us with a love that is unquenchable. Remember what Jeremiah taught us, that Adonai loves us with an eternal love" (31:3).

This arresting image of a divine love so powerful, so enduring that it supersedes even parental love was taken up by one of the psalmists who, at his time of despair, cried out,

Do not forsake me; do not abandon me, O God, my deliverer.
Though my father and mother might abandon me,
Adonai will take me in. (Ps. 27:9-10)

Throughout the Bible and the subsequent liturgy that draws so heavily on Psalms and the prophets, there are reminders of the deep and abiding love that God has for the people of Israel. But nowhere is that theme more poignantly expressed than in D-Isaiah's assurance that the love of Adonai for His covenanted people is deeper even than that of a mother for "the child of her womb." But as beautiful and heartfelt as the prophet's words were, the people were not ready to accept them. They were so grievously demoralized by the destruction, the temple in flames, the exile, the poverty, and starvation that they could not be mollified by the words of a messenger, a mere agent of God. They needed the comfort of God directly without an intermediary. And it was that need, as perceived by the Judaean sages about five centuries later, that led to one of the most remarkable liturgical traditions in Judaism.

The liturgy of the synagogue prescribes the reading of certain haftarot (selections from the prophets that are read following the weekly Torah readings) at Shabbat services for three weeks prior to and seven weeks following the fast day which is called *Tisha b'Ab* (the Ninth Day of the month of Ab). *Tisha b'Ab* memorializes the destruction of the Temple in Jerusalem (based on dating in Jeremiah and 2 Kings), and it is by far the most mournful day on the Jewish calendar. Later traditions have it that the Second Temple was destroyed on that same day and that other tragedies in Jewish history (most notably the expulsion of the Jews from Spain) also occurred on *Tisha b'Ab*. But the traditions and liturgy of *Tisha b'Ab* derive from the destruction of 587-86 BCE.

The prescription for the reading of these ten pre- and post-*Tisha b'Ab* haftarot goes back to at least the first century and has served as a sort of collective catharsis for Jewish communities since then as they recalled tragedies both ancient and contemporary. The three haftarot that are prescribed for the weeks before *Tisha b'Ab* are prophecies of *tochaha* (rebuke and warning). The first two are from Jeremiah (Excerpts: *"From the north shall disaster break loose upon all the inhabitants of the land!"* [1:14] and *"My people have done a two-fold wrong: they have forsaken Me, the fount of living waters, and hewed them out cisterns, broken cisterns, which cannot hold water"* [2:13].).

The third and climactic prophecy of *tochaha* is read on the Sabbath just before *Tisha b'Ab*. That Sabbath is called *Shabbat Hazon*, the Sabbath of the Vision, referring to the dire vision of Isaiah that includes these rebukes and warnings:

> *Ah, sinful nation! People laden with iniquity! Brood of evildoers! Depraved children! They have forsaken Adonai, spurned the Holy One of Israel, . . .*

> *Fair Zion is left like a booth in a vineyard, like a hut in a cucumber field, like a city beleaguered. Had not Adonai Tzevaot left us some survivors, we should be like Sodom, another Gomorrah.*

> *Alas, she has become a harlot, the faithful city that was filled with justice, where righteousness dwelt—but now murderers.* (1:4, 8-9, 21)

That haftarah serves as prelude to the mournful fast day of *Tisha b'Av* with its dirges and the reading of the scroll of Lamentations. But then comes the *Sheva d'Nehamta*, the Seven Prophecies of Consolation, all taken from the twenty-six chapters of D-Isaiah that were appended to the book of Isaiah. These seven prophecies are read on the seven Sabbaths that separate Tisha b'Ab from Rosh ha-Shanah, the Jewish New Year. The first of those seven Sabbaths is called *Shabbat Nahamu*, the Sabbath on which the haftarah begins with these words, directed to the prophet.

> *Nahamu nahamu ami—Comfort, oh comfort My people, says your God.*
> *Speak tenderly to Jerusalem, and declare to her*
> *that her term of service is over, that her iniquity is expiated;*
> *for she has received from the hand of Adonai double for all her sins.*

This first of the *Sheva d'Nehamta* sets the task for the prophet. He is directed to find the right words that will bind up the wounds, that will convince the decimated people that their God yet lives, loves them, and has marked them for a sacred and universal task. One might have expected that the first-century sages who established the order of the haftarot would simply have chosen the most comforting utterances of D-Isaiah, following the directive to the prophet to comfort the people, to *"speak tenderly to Jerusalem."* But they went further. They chose an order of seven prophecies, the opening verses of which would constitute a dialogue, first, between God and the prophet; second, between the prophet and the people; and finally, between God and the people.

Here is that dialogue, as chanted in the synagogue every week for the past two thousand years on the seven Sabbaths following, as it were, the Destruction:

Week 1—Isaiah 40:1-26
God addresses the prophet:

> *Comfort, oh comfort my people, . . . Speak tenderly to Jerusalem . . .*

Week 2—Isaiah 49:14-51:3
The prophet, hearing the people complaining that God has forgotten and forsaken them, addresses the people:

> *Can a woman forget her baby, or disown the child of her womb?*
> *Though she might forget, I never could forget you.*

Week 3—Isaiah 54:11-55:5
The prophet recognizes that no matter how poignant and empathetic his words, the people will not be comforted by a human messenger:

> *Unhappy, storm-tossed one, uncomforted!*

Week 4—Isaiah 51:12-52:12
God relieves the prophet of the task of reviving the people. No human agency will suffice. And so God speaks to them directly, reminding them of the divine omnipotence:

> *I, I am the One who comforts you! What ails you that you fear man who*
> *must die? . . . You have forgotten Adonai, your Maker, who stretched*
> *out the skies and made firm the earth.*

Week 5—Isaiah 54:1-10
God continues personally to encourage the people, assuring them that, having been punished, their future is glorious:

> *Shout, O barren one, you who bore no child!*
> *Shout aloud for joy, you who did not travail!*
> *For the children of the wife forlorn shall outnumber those of the*
> *espoused.*

Enlarge the site of your tent, . . . do not stint!
For you shall spread out to the right and the left;
Your offspring shall dispossess nations . . .

Week 6—Isaiah 60

Recognizing that the people have now accepted the personal reassurances of God, the prophet returns to the dialogue and joins the people in their revival:

Arise, shine, for your light has dawned;
the presence of Adonai has shone upon you!
Behold! Darkness shall cover the earth, and thick clouds the peoples;
But upon you, Adonai shall shine, and His presence be seen over you.
And nations shall walk by your light, kings by your shining radiance.

Week 7—Isaiah 61:10-63:9

The dialogue concludes as the people express their gratitude to God, not only for reviving them but for restoring them to a position of honor among the nations:

I greatly rejoice in Adonai, my whole being exults in my God.
For He has clothed me with garments of triumph, wrapped me in a robe of victory.
. . . Adonai will make victory and renown shoot up in the presence of all the nations.

What better preparation could there be for the High Holy Days than the prophetic lessons that are read on the ten Sabbaths that precede Rosh ha-Shanah? For three weeks, congregants listen to the dire warnings of the consequences of sin. Then, inexorably, comes the punishment for disobedience: the utter destruction of *Tisha b'Av*. But that is quickly followed by the binding up of the wounds, by repeated reassurances of the grace of God. The lesson is clear: God gave the commandments to Israel so that we might live by them, not only for our own sake but for the sake of humanity that Israel might be "a light to the nations."

There may be times when everything looks bleak, when the task given to Israel by God seems impossible, and the temptations to slough off responsibility are too great to resist. At those times, it might seem as if God has deserted us, that God has been removed from the arc of Jewish history. But no, that could never happen: *"Can a woman forget her baby, or disown the child of her womb? Though she might forget, I could never forget you."*

Every year when I hear the chanting of those poignantly penetrating words, I close my eyes and see God sitting on a low mourning stool, holding the hands of bereaved Israel, crying together with Mother Rachel. And from those shared tears, there blossoms the resolve to take up the task again, with renewed vigor, to be a light to the nations so that God's blessings might extend to every nation on earth. And I am prepared to enter into the New Year with the faith that, indeed, *"Adonai will make victory and renown shoot up in the presence of the nations."*

Turn 11

Let us make man in our image.

—*Genesis 1:26*

Virtually every Bible scholar, from rabbinic apologete to trinitarian fundamentalist, has had a go at the divine declaration that climaxes the final day of Creation: "*Let us make man in our image, in our likeness.*" To whom was God speaking? Who are the "us"? Were there heavenly courtiers or angels? Was God employing the plural of royalty? Was the Father speaking to the Son and the Holy Spirit? These questions are underscored by the fact that we find this same paradoxical usage in two other early Genesis verses, 3:22 and 11:7. In all three cases, God seems to be discussing the divine plan for humanity with others.

I find all such speculation about as meaningful as the scores of impassioned medieval opinions about the number of angels that can fit on the head of a pin. A much more basic question is, Does God speak to anyone at all, celestial or human? Isn't the idea of a speaking god just another example of the kind of anthropomorphism that one might expect from an age when humanity was just beginning its very long journey from paganism to monotheism? The biblical narrator had to explain what it was that God was planning. How better to explain than to have God announce the divine intention?

I have no interest in defending the unity of a god who speaks in the first person plural. That is not the reason why I find this verse to be so compelling. I gladly leave all speculation as to the deeper meaning of "us" and "our" to those who are not capable of severing that powerfully venerable umbilicus that binds so many "believers" to idolatry. My interest in this verse, a verse that I consider to be at the very heart of ethical monotheism, is the concept of the Creation of human beings in the image of God. What does it mean to be created in the divine image? What was really on the mind of that ancient genius who first conceived of God declaring, "*Naaseh adam b'tzalmenu* (Let us make man in our image)."

Before proceeding to delve into the mind of that religious prodigy, it might be wise to clear away any misunderstanding about the word *image* or the word that follows on its heels, "*d'mutenu* (our likeness)." Although we find many references in the Bible to the anatomy of God (see especially Exod. 33:19-23 where the text refers to God's face, hand, and back), it is clear that the authors were employing language that could be readily understood by people who were not very far removed from paganism. This unique mammal that God fashioned as the culmination of the creative process stood erect; it could speak; it could create and utilize fire and tools; it could transmit ideas to its children; it could conceive of a mysteriously powerful imminence; ergo, it was in some way like that mysterious being, "in the image" of that being.

There is an interesting statement by the third-century Babylonian sage, Rav Hamnuna, suggesting that a person who prays on the eve of Shabbat and recites "*Va-yechulu*" (the opening paragraph of Genesis, chapter 2: "*The heaven and the earth were finished . . . And God blessed the seventh day and declared it holy, because on it God ceased from all the work of creation*") that such a person is considered as if he were a partner with God in the work of Creation (Tractate *Shabbat* 119b).

That phrase, "a partner with God in the work of creation," is certainly one of the most startling and compelling in all of rabbinic literature. We find it again earlier in tractate *Shabbat* where Rav Hiyya explains to two colleagues whose practice it was to sit in judgment for the entire day until they were exhausted: "A judge who judges his fellows fairly just for one hour, such a person is considered as if he were a partner with God in the work of creation" (Tractate *Shabbat* 10a). The great medieval commentator, Rashi, repeats this idea of potential human partnership with God in his commentary on Exodus 18:13, and many Jewish theologians down through the ages have employed that same usage to further explain what is meant by "*created in the image of God.*"

The ancient storyteller who first bestowed that encomium on humanity recognized, whether intuitively or presciently, that God the Creator had left a lot yet to be done, that the Creation was only potentially perfect. The human being could gather the seeds which were a gift from God, but he had to plant them and nourish them in order to reap the reward of bread. The human being could wonder at the multitude of animals, fishes, and fowls that shared the world with him; but he had to select and domesticate some of them in order utilize them for food or for aid in labor. And at a later stage, the human being, beset by illness and plague, came to realize that God had created herbs and minerals and, yes, the wisdom that might enable him to use these divine gifts in order to cure those scourges.

To recognize that one is created in the image of God is to recognize at the same time that this "image," whatever it might be, makes us capable of partnership with God:

- That as God is powerful, so we are created with powers that can be used for the benefit of God's children.

- That as God is the loving source of life, so are we capable, through acts of love, of creating life.

- That as God is the Creator of all human beings—rich and poor, black and white, whole and broken—so it is our responsibility to share God's resources with all human beings.

- That as God is omniscient, so are we endowed with the wisdom to educate our children, to cure the sick, to establish courts of justice, and to create music and art.

One of my favorites among the brilliant cadre of contemporary Israeli novelists is Aharon Appelfeld. A few years ago, on the sixtieth anniversary of the liberation of Auschwitz, he wrote an op-ed piece for the *New York Times* (1/27/05) describing the state of mind of the pitiful remnant, himself among them, who survived. He concluded his essay by quoting the remark of a fellow survivor, a doctor who in 1946 sailed with him from Italy to Israel:

> We didn't see God when we expected him, so we have no choice
> but to do what he was supposed to do: we will protect the weak,
> we will love, we will comfort. From now on, the responsibility is
> all ours.

That same idea was expressed in a cartoon that I remember seeing many years ago. Two men are having a deep conversation about life. Man A says to Man B, "I would like to ask God why He allows so many people to suffer from illness and poverty." Man B says, "Well, why don't you?" And Man A answers, "I'm afraid God might ask me the same question."

Both Appelfeld's fellow survivor and Man A in the cartoon were expressing the same idea: that as partners of God, it is our responsibility to take up the work where God has, for whatever metaphysical reason, left off. One of the deepest elements of my faith is that just as God has provided the inspiration for music and literature and art, so God has provided the solution for every ill that ever has or ever will beset humanity. An old Yiddish proverb has it that before God creates the plague, God creates the cure. It is our task, as the partners of God, to find that cure.

Am I being simplistic? I don't think so. How explain the fact that while hundreds of thousands of God's creatures are dying of starvation in Africa, grain storehouses in America are bursting with plenty? How explain the fact that while our planet is choking on emissions of all sorts, factories go on producing monstrous toxin-spewing motor vehicles? How explain the fact that in this "land of the free," some receive educations and medical care that enable them to enjoy the blessings of freedom while fellow citizens in this richest nation on earth are mired in something akin to slavery? These and hundreds of other "plagues" of our time are capable of solution, of acts of partnership with the God in whose image we are created. The divinely created solution is readily available to us, but . . .

I hope that my readers do not consider it a blasphemy for me to confess that I do not believe in the so-called miracles of the Bible. Actually, I do believe in miracles. I believe that each baby born is a potential miracle, I believe that the Bach Cello Suites and Michelangelo's *Pieta* and Shakespeare's *King Lear* are miracles, I believe that the prophecies of Isaiah and the book of Job are miracles, I believe that the brilliance of Einstein and the compassion of Gandhi are miracles. All of these are expressions of divinity that emerged from mortals who were inspired to transcend the mundane and reach out for the sublime. These are miracles.

But I do not believe that God split the sea for the Israelites, I do not believe that God sent down fire at the behest of Elijah, I do not believe that Elisha brought a dead child back to life. I find these stories to be charming and even instructive, and I realize that I am part of a people that has been telling these stories for millennia and that has been influenced by them. But no, as historical facts, they never happened. And that brings us to Sinai.

What happened at Mt. Sinai? It is impossible to reconstruct the history of Israel from patriarchal times to the creation of a commonwealth in the land of Canaan. There is no independent record, archaeological or otherwise, to support the notion that at a particular moment twelve tribes who had recently escaped from Egyptian bondage received the Law from God at a mountain in the wilderness. That Israel has possessed all or some of the Torah since antiquity is beyond question, that the Torah is the inerrant word of God is, I regret to say, quite questionable. I will not attempt to list all of the anomalies in the Torah that make it impossible for a critical, scientifically educated person to believe that the Torah in its entirety is "the Word of God." I offer just a few examples:

- God never commanded that a woman suspected of adultery be subjected to a trial by ordeal and possible execution.

- God never commanded the holocaust of multitudes of animals so that their sweet savor might be enjoyed in heaven.

- God never commanded a father to slaughter his son, whether as a trial of faith or for any other savage reason.

- God never caused the earth to open and swallow a part of the camp of Israel.

- God never caused a serpent to speak to a woman or a donkey to speak to its master.

Yes, I believe in the Torah. I consider it a blessing to be able to teach Torah; and I delight in singing out in the midst of a congregation each Shabbat morning, "*Baruch she-natan Torah l'amo Yisrael* (Blessed is the One who gave the Torah to our people Israel)." I believe in the Torah as a divinely inspired text, *most of which* teaches an ethic which has yet to be realized by humanity. But I believe also that it is the task of the true God-believer to examine every verse of that Torah in order to extract that which is "of God" and that which is a product of misunderstanding. I learned from Martin Buber that "an observant Jew . . . when he has to choose between God and the Bible, chooses God." (See essay on Samuel and Agag) If we find in our study of Torah that which contradicts our belief in a just and merciful God, then it is our responsibility as lovers of Torah and as lovers of God to recognize it as a misunderstanding and to "choose God."

Israel did, at some early point in its history, experience a theophany, a liberating awareness of God that inspires ethical living. The who, what, when, where, and how of that theophany are shrouded in mystery. The Torah is neither a history book nor a journal, and so we should not be surprised that it offers a mythology of that theophany.

At some point, probably during the early monarchy, an inspired religious prodigy gathered together the traditions of several tribes, refashioned them magnificently, and ascribed a time and place for the revelation of God's Torah. The time: the ministry of Moses; the place: Mount Sinai. But the time and place are of no consequence. What *is* of consequence is that, as the result of unique circumstances, Israel saw itself as pledged to God, as chosen to live "*in the image of God.*" Ever since, this awareness that God communicates the divine will to humanity has been referred to as "Mount Sinai."

The American critic and novelist Cynthia Ozick in her novel *Heir to the Glimmering World* has one of her characters declare, "At Sinai the minds of men were given the power to read the mind of God." That is as brilliant a statement of the meaning of Sinai as any that I have encountered. Human beings were gifted by God with the power to look beyond the confines of their individual lives, beyond even the interests of their particular families and tribes, and to recognize that they might join their lives to a perpetually creative power whose purpose is *shalom*—completeness, the liberation and ennoblement of every human being. "At Sinai the minds of men were given the power to read the mind of God." Thus are we created "*in the image of God.*" We have within us the divine gift that makes it possible for us "*l'taken olam* (to perfect the world)."

> *Beloved of God is humanity, created in the image of God; but an even greater love moved God to cause humans to realize that they were created in the image of God.* (Pirke Avot [*Sayings of the Fathers*] 3:18)

Turn 12

*Though my father and my
mother abandon me,
Adonai will take me in.*

—*Psalms 27:10*

As a child, I often felt unwanted, as if I were an orphan who had somehow been abandoned by his parents. With the years, I have come to understand that most children have similar feelings at various times and that, although my parents were away from home more often than not, it was not for lack of love and concern. They were heavily involved in community affairs, and that meant that I spent a lot of time alone in a creaky sixteen-room old house. Solitude often led to mischief, mischief to punishment, and punishment to a reinforcement of my feelings of unwantedness.

Fortunately, one of the rooms in that big old house was a library, well-stocked with the classics and Jewish sacred literature but eclectic enough to include such profanities as the *Decameron* and *Forever Amber*. I devoured them all, voraciously, uncritically, and occasionally guiltily. Books were my best friends and my refuge during the many solitary hours of my early teen years, until . . . until . . .

I was sent away from our suburban Boston home to New York to study at the Yeshiva University high school. There, I felt not only unwanted but abandoned. Unlike my home where I could find refuge, and even titillation, in my father's library, the yeshiva high school library contained only sacred literature and assigned high school texts. Those therapeutic hours that I had spent sitting in a cozy corner of the library at home were replaced in New York for two years by stolen hours at one of the four movie houses on 181st Street or by sitting in my dorm room devising stratagems to convince my parents to let me come home. (My winning ploy was to convince my mother that the dorm was a hotbed of homosexual activity. Yes, the pun is intentional and yes, I was guilty of exaggeration . . . slightly.) Victorious, I spent my final precollege years at our hometown high school.

But as eager as I was to put the yeshiva with all of its burdensome pieties behind me, I confess that I learned more in those two years than during any other similar period in my life. I actually tried *not* to learn. I would hide the tabloid *PM* in my Talmud folio and avidly absorb left-wing politics rather than the dicta of Abbaye and Rava; I would use the intertextual margins of the folio pages to flick spitballs here and there in simulated baseball games; I would claim not to understand Yiddish, the language of instruction in our Talmud classes. On one occasion when my father came to New York to inquire from my rebbe about the progress of his *ben yochid* (his only son), I received the most superlative encomium of my young life: "*Aza niet vellen lernen hob ich nisht in mein leben gezen!* (Such an unwillingness to learn I have never in my life seen!)" But learn I did, somehow, it may have been osmosis. I was there, and I absorbed—unwittingly and unwillingly.

What was it that I absorbed? For one thing, a familiarity with the cadences of the Aramaic texts. The subject matter may have eluded this young teenager, but when I returned to Talmudic studies, at Harvard with Professor Harry Wolfson and then at Hebrew Union College, I found that I was comfortable with rabbinic texts. I had the basic vocabulary; I could appreciate nuance; and I quickly came to understand the historic and sociological *sitz in leben* of the sages, something which was ignored in the yeshiva world.

But there was something else that I absorbed even more so during those two yeshiva years, and that was a familiarity with Jewish liturgy. At home, my father used to take me to synagogue whenever it did not interfere with school and whenever he could find me at prayer times, and so I knew most of the standard daily and Sabbath liturgy by heart even before I left for New York. But at the yeshiva attendance at the three daily services was mandatory. I cannot recall missing a *Shaharit* or a *Minhah* or a *Maariv* during the two years of my residence at the dorm; it was required, and absence for whatever reason meant an unpleasant hour with the *mashgiah ruhni* (the spiritual guide). Which brings me to *L'Dovid Ori* . . .

I arrived in New York to begin my studies at yeshiva on Labor Day, 1944, about two weeks before the High Holy Days; and I found out on that very first day that attendance at services was not optional. I was resignedly unpacking my bag in the dorm room when an older boy came in and asked rather belligerently why I wasn't at *Minhah*. It took me a moment to understand what he was saying, and I stammered some answer indicating that I didn't

m grateful that I was not familiar with this commentary by Rashi w
was feeling abandoned in New York at the tender age of fourteen. A
th all due respect for Rashi, I feel confident that Rashi's interpretation
furthest thing from the mind of the psalmist when he first chanted t
ignant verse. What I know for certain is that Psalm 27 was revealed
when I needed it. I survived and indeed, flourished during the two yea
my "exile" at least in part because I had my mantra, because I knew th
ough my father and mother might have abandoned me, Adonai would tak
in. We have been good friends ever since.

know where there was a shul. He asked me how I could be so dumb, grabbed me by the hand, and led me to the *beis medresh*, the large study hall which doubled as a synagogue for daily services. *Minhah* was almost over, but I knew enough to take a siddur, sit down, and wait for *Maariv*.

One of the college students chanted the service rather perfunctorily, pretty much in the manner that I was used to from those rare occasions when I attended a weekday service at home. Then after the Kaddish, when I thought that the service was over, one of the rabbis sitting near the pulpit called out, "*L'Dovid Ori*," and everyone around me answered by zipping through a psalm that I did not recognize. The prayer leader then chanted the concluding words and there followed another Kaddish. And that concluded the service.

I didn't want to admit my ignorance by asking someone what *L'Dovid Ori* was, and so the next morning at *Shaharit*, I stole a glance at the page of the siddur in the hands of the fellow next to me and I turned to that page. There, I found that they were reading Psalm 27 which begins with the Hebrew words "*L'David Adonai ori* (Of David: Adonai is my light and my salvation)." This psalm is traditionally prescribed for reading at the conclusion of all morning and evening services for the entire month leading up to Rosh ha-Shanah and continuing through most of the Sukkot holiday. And so it was that during the first month of my enforced exile from home and family, twice each day I joined in chanting the unfamiliar Psalm 27.

It was in that psalm that I found the mantra that perfectly expressed my state of mind during those two dismal years in New York: "*Ki avi v'imi azavuni* (Though my father and mother abandon me, Adonai will take me in)." I had been abandoned, left in a hostile environment two hundred miles from family, friends, and library, and twice a day during that crucial first month of my abandonment, my feelings were underscored by the sacred text that I chanted along with the congregation. "*Though my father and mother abandon me . . . though my father and mother abandon me . . . though my father and mother abandon me . . .*" I have long since overcome that feeling of abandonment, but still today I feel tears welling up inside every time I hear a gospel singer crooning, "*Sometimes I feel like a motherless child.*"

As might be obvious from this collection of biblical verses that have penetrated my soul and that I in turn seek to penetrate, there are passages from virtually every book in the Bible that pop into my mind, unbidden, at any time, day or night. Again, I return to those two years in the yeshiva. I had a Bible teacher, Rav Riger, whom I recall for his kindness and his love for the language of the prophets. But kind as he was, he believed that there was only one way to really appreciate the words of Amos, Isaiah, Jeremiah, and the Psalms and that was to commit them to memory. And so every class began with rote recitations by classmates of long passages that we had been required to memorize.

Needless to say, I hated those daily exercises of rote repetition, but I value them deeply today. And I realize now that the passages that run most frequently through my mind—and that Rav Riger must have cherished in particular—have to do with God's fulfilling the parental role, with God's love matching or exceeding that of mother or father. There are many of them: Psalms 103:13, Ezekiel 16:4-14, Jeremiah 31:20 come readily to mind. The theology that I have evolved over the years rests solidly on those passages, on the idea of God's empathetic presence for those in need. I don't expect miracles from God; I expect and feel kinship, as if Adonai were my metamother/father, the one upon whom I can depend to "take me in" when I feel abandoned.

It was while writing about one of those passages, "*Can a woman forget her baby or abandon the child of her womb?*" (Isa. 49:15), that I was moved to think about other passages that refer to God's love in the face of abandonment by parents. And the one that came most readily to mind was that personal mantra from my years of, as I understood it, abandonment: "*Though my father and mother abandon me, Adonai will take me in.*" That verse helped me not only to endure those two years of exile but also to keep my mind open. I may have exhibited a unique "unwillingness to learn," but learn I did because of that innate security that flowed from the assurance that under the worst of circumstances God would "take me in," that God was nearby.

And so I decided to revisit that cherished verse and to see what the rabbinic commentators had to say about it. I began—and ended!!—with the preeminent Bible commentator, Rashi (Rabbi Solomon b. Isaac, eleventh century France). Rashi is known for his terse and usually literal interpretations of sacred text. He used midrashic material when he thought that it might amplify a verse, but he rarely strayed from that which was clearly implicit. And so his interpretation of Psalms 27:10 is shocking, to say the least.

Though my father and mother abandon me—During the intercourse for their pleasure, they determined that after the enjoyed themselves, he would turn away to his side and she w turn to her side [i.e., *coitus interruptus* so that the ejaculate n not enter and impregnate her] . . .

Adonai will take me in—The Holy One, blessed be He, guards recovers] the sperm and preserves the embryo.

What could possibly have been on Rashi's mind when he decid future generations with this bit of "prolife" propaganda? Was teaching us that God was opposed to the wasting of sperm thwart attempts by couples to enjoy sex for its own sake, i.e., w intention of conception? He certainly had ample grounds to opin disapproved of the wasting of seed; remember the story of Onan And while there is no explicit prohibition against coitus interrup the marital relationship in the Bible or the early rabbinic literature, enough opposition to it in the rabbinic academies of Rashi's era an to conjecture that he might have opposed the practice.

I would, though, offer a different interpretation of Rashi's startling c We know that, in addition to his encyclopedic knowledge of Jewish so was a man of broad experience. His commentaries reveal a familiarity many aspects of daily life, both Jewish and Christian, in the society of I suggest that through both personal experience and the conventional of his day, he knew that coitus interruptus was not a very effective of birth control. He may not have been totally familiar with the phy that enables sperm to arrive at its natural target even unintentionally, certainly was aware that pregnancy often occurred in those circumsta

What Rashi was teaching us, I believe, was the lesson that we find folklore of virtually every culture since it first appeared in the book of Pr 19:21: "*Many thoughts are in the mind of man, but it is God's plan accomplished.*" You may have heard it as "man proposes but God dis or as "*Der mensch tracht und Gott lacht.*" I feel confident that Rashi wa teaching us that marital sex without the intention of conception was evil seems to me very uncharacteristic of Rashi. What he was teaching us rat that sexual relations often lead to pregnancy, whether or not intended.

know where there was a shul. He asked me how I could be so dumb, grabbed me by the hand, and led me to the *beis medresh*, the large study hall which doubled as a synagogue for daily services. *Minhah* was almost over, but I knew enough to take a siddur, sit down, and wait for *Maariv*.

One of the college students chanted the service rather perfunctorily, pretty much in the manner that I was used to from those rare occasions when I attended a weekday service at home. Then after the Kaddish, when I thought that the service was over, one of the rabbis sitting near the pulpit called out, "*L'Dovid Ori*," and everyone around me answered by zipping through a psalm that I did not recognize. The prayer leader then chanted the concluding words and there followed another Kaddish. And that concluded the service.

I didn't want to admit my ignorance by asking someone what *L'Dovid Ori* was, and so the next morning at *Shaharit*, I stole a glance at the page of the siddur in the hands of the fellow next to me and I turned to that page. There, I found that they were reading Psalm 27 which begins with the Hebrew words "*L'David Adonai ori* (Of David: Adonai is my light and my salvation)." This psalm is traditionally prescribed for reading at the conclusion of all morning and evening services for the entire month leading up to Rosh ha-Shanah and continuing through most of the Sukkot holiday. And so it was that during the first month of my enforced exile from home and family, twice each day I joined in chanting the unfamiliar Psalm 27.

It was in that psalm that I found the mantra that perfectly expressed my state of mind during those two dismal years in New York: "*Ki avi v'imi azavuni* (Though my father and mother abandon me, Adonai will take me in)." I had been abandoned, left in a hostile environment two hundred miles from family, friends, and library, and twice a day during that crucial first month of my abandonment, my feelings were underscored by the sacred text that I chanted along with the congregation. "*Though my father and mother abandon me . . . though my father and mother abandon me . . . though my father and mother abandon me . . .*" I have long since overcome that feeling of abandonment, but still today I feel tears welling up inside every time I hear a gospel singer crooning, "*Sometimes I feel like a motherless child.*"

As might be obvious from this collection of biblical verses that have penetrated my soul and that I in turn seek to penetrate, there are passages from virtually every book in the Bible that pop into my mind, unbidden, at any time, day or night. Again, I return to those two years in the yeshiva. I had a Bible teacher, Rav Riger, whom I recall for his kindness and his love for the language of the prophets. But kind as he was, he believed that there was only one way to really appreciate the words of Amos, Isaiah, Jeremiah, and the Psalms and that was to commit them to memory. And so every class began with rote recitations by classmates of long passages that we had been required to memorize.

Needless to say, I hated those daily exercises of rote repetition, but I value them deeply today. And I realize now that the passages that run most frequently through my mind—and that Rav Riger must have cherished in particular—have to do with God's fulfilling the parental role, with God's love matching or exceeding that of mother or father. There are many of them: Psalms 103:13, Ezekiel 16:4-14, Jeremiah 31:20 come readily to mind. The theology that I have evolved over the years rests solidly on those passages, on the idea of God's empathetic presence for those in need. I don't expect miracles from God; I expect and feel kinship, as if Adonai were my metamother/father, the one upon whom I can depend to "take me in" when I feel abandoned.

It was while writing about one of those passages, *"Can a woman forget her baby or abandon the child of her womb?"* (Isa. 49:15), that I was moved to think about other passages that refer to God's love in the face of abandonment by parents. And the one that came most readily to mind was that personal mantra from my years of, as I understood it, abandonment: *"Though my father and mother abandon me, Adonai will take me in."* That verse helped me not only to endure those two years of exile but also to keep my mind open. I may have exhibited a unique "unwillingness to learn," but learn I did because of that innate security that flowed from the assurance that under the worst of circumstances God would "take me in," that God was nearby.

And so I decided to revisit that cherished verse and to see what the rabbinic commentators had to say about it. I began—and ended!!—with the preeminent Bible commentator, Rashi (Rabbi Solomon b. Isaac, eleventh century France). Rashi is known for his terse and usually literal interpretations of sacred text. He used midrashic material when he thought that it might amplify a verse, but he rarely strayed from that which was clearly implicit. And so his interpretation of Psalms 27:10 is shocking, to say the least.

Though my father and mother abandon me—During the act of intercourse for their pleasure, they determined that after they had enjoyed themselves, he would turn away to his side and she would turn to her side [i.e., *coitus interruptus* so that the ejaculate might not enter and impregnate her] . . .

Adonai will take me in—The Holy One, blessed be He, guards [i.e., recovers] the sperm and preserves the embryo.

What could possibly have been on Rashi's mind when he decided to favor future generations with this bit of "prolife" propaganda? Was he, in fact, teaching us that God was opposed to the wasting of sperm and would thwart attempts by couples to enjoy sex for its own sake, i.e., without the intention of conception? He certainly had ample grounds to opine that God disapproved of the wasting of seed; remember the story of Onan (Gen. 38). And while there is no explicit prohibition against coitus interruptus within the marital relationship in the Bible or the early rabbinic literature, there was enough opposition to it in the rabbinic academies of Rashi's era and beyond to conjecture that he might have opposed the practice.

I would, though, offer a different interpretation of Rashi's startling comment. We know that, in addition to his encyclopedic knowledge of Jewish sources, he was a man of broad experience. His commentaries reveal a familiarity with the many aspects of daily life, both Jewish and Christian, in the society of his day. I suggest that through both personal experience and the conventional wisdom of his day, he knew that coitus interruptus was not a very effective method of birth control. He may not have been totally familiar with the physiology that enables sperm to arrive at its natural target even unintentionally, but he certainly was aware that pregnancy often occurred in those circumstances.

What Rashi was teaching us, I believe, was the lesson that we find in the folklore of virtually every culture since it first appeared in the book of Proverbs 19:21: *"Many thoughts are in the mind of man, but it is God's plan that is accomplished."* You may have heard it as "man proposes but God disposes" or as *"Der mensch tracht und Gott lacht."* I feel confident that Rashi was not teaching us that marital sex without the intention of conception was evil; that seems to me very uncharacteristic of Rashi. What he was teaching us rather is that sexual relations often lead to pregnancy, whether or not intended.

I am grateful that I was not familiar with this commentary by Rashi when I was feeling abandoned in New York at the tender age of fourteen. And with all due respect for Rashi, I feel confident that Rashi's interpretation was the furthest thing from the mind of the psalmist when he first chanted that poignant verse. What I know for certain is that Psalm 27 was revealed to me when I needed it. I survived and indeed, flourished during the two years of my "exile" at least in part because I had my mantra, because I knew that though my father and mother might have abandoned me, Adonai would take me in. We have been good friends ever since.

Turn 13

*A lion has roared,
who can but fear?*

—Amos 3:8

I have made reference elsewhere ("*Though my father and mother abandon me . . .*") to Rav Riger, my Bible teacher at the yeshiva high school and to his favorite pedagogical method, memorization. And since he had a particular love for the book of Amos, one should not be surprised to learn that at the age of fourteen, I had committed the entire book to memory, as assigned. Actually, that is not as impressive as it sounds. The book of Amos has only nine chapters, and most of those chapters are not only lyrical but they speak to the soul, even the callow soul, that delights in a rustic Jewish hero who defies authority. Add to that the yearning for social justice that was so common among Jewish adolescents raised during the Depression, and you will understand that by the time that I had completed Rav Riger's assignment, I too loved Amos.

Years later, at Hebrew Union College, I would learn that only about half of the nine chapters of Amos are actually the words of the eloquent eighth-pre-Christian century farmer-prophet. At the yeshiva, it would have been heresy even to suggest that Amos or any other book of the Bible was not spoken or written in toto by its traditional author, from the "Torah of Moses" on. But I was introduced to biblical criticism at HUC, and while I might differ with this or that element of the documentary theory—i.e., that a variety of ancient texts from various times were woven together and edited to arrive at the Masoretic or traditional text that is considered sacred among Jews today—I have no doubt that it is substantially true.

I was probably the only student who ever came to HUC knowing the book of Amos by heart; and so, as I studied it anew with Professor Sheldon Blank, I learned to deal with it (and with the other books of the Bible) on two levels: first, on the level of the text as a sacred unity received intact from previous generations, and second, on the level of the text as an amalgam of documents from several different inspired sources beginning with the putative author, in this case Amos, and including also prophetic fragments from later authors who felt that they were improving on or elucidating the original text.

To illustrate these two approaches, let's take a look at chapter one of Amos. After a brief biographical verse identifying Amos as a prophet who came from Judah to preach against the sins of the Northern Kingdom, Israel, and after a powerful opening statement of God's impending vengeance, the prophet goes on to a series of denouncements of the unrighteous acts of seven different nations, all enemies of Israel. Most critical scholars agree that the authentic prophesies of Amos begin with chapter 2, verse 6, with his verbal onslaught against Israel and that what we find before that are a series of oracles against enemies of Israel, in the style of the book of Obadiah, composed by some later author who felt that if God instructed Amos to cry out against the heinous sins of Israel and Judah, His own children, then He must have instructed him also to cry out against the even more heinous sins of the idolatrous nations.

If we, though, like Rav Riger, are inclined to the first level of understanding mentioned above—i.e., the unity of the text—one might make a case that the prophet was employing a clever stratagem, that he began his message by attacking the enemies of Israel, working the crowd into an empathetic frenzy, before getting to the point: the sins of Israel. His final denouncement, before getting to the excoriation of Israel, was of Judah, his own homeland and the primary rival of Israel. How delighted the mob must have been with his crescendo:

> *I will send down fire upon Judah,*
> *and it shall devour the fortresses of Jerusalem.*

As Rav Riger explained to us, the crowd would have been cheering wildly, egging Amos on. After his increasingly bitter attacks on Damascus, Gaza, Tyre, Edom, Ammon, and Moab, he gave passionate voice to their resentment of their Judean cousins who claimed that the Israelite sanctuary at Bethel was illegitimate, that God could be worshipped only in Judean Jerusalem. Here was a Judean, claiming to speak for God, announcing that Jerusalem would be destroyed. He had the crowd in the palm of his hand and then . . .

Each of the oracles against the enemy nations is uttered in two or three verses, each beginning with the formulaic: *"For the three sins of . . . , for four I will not revoke it"* followed by the itemization of those multiple sins. Then, having finished with Judah, he starts again:

For the three transgressions of Israel, and for four I will not revoke it . . .

There must have been a gasp from the crowd—*How dare he!!*—and then silence as the prophet, this rude Judean farmer, probably dressed in homespun, began his tirade against the iniquities of Israel. He would go on for eleven powerful verses, not the two or three directed against enemies that had been so enthusiastically lapped up by the Bethel crowd. I can hear the people recovering their voices and beginning to jeer as he catalogues their misdeeds. But they certainly heard at least the first three or four verses of Amos's attack, and those are the most biting and powerful:

> *Because they have sold the just for silver,*
> *and the needy for a pair of sandals.*
> *You who trample the heads of the poor into the dust,*
> *and push the humble of the land off the road.*
> *Father and son go to the same girl,*
> *and thereby profane My holy name.*
> *They recline on every altar on garments taken in pledge,*
> *and drink in the house of their God wine bought with fines they imposed.*

Whether you go along with Rav Riger and the traditionalists who read the entire book as the words of Amos or you winnow out that which the historic Amos is actually likely to have said from the addenda of other prophets, Amos's blunt denunciations of the Israelites' violations of their sacred covenant of justice with God are the essence of this thin but riveting book.

That I might one day decide to abandon the Orthodox Jewish emphasis on ritual in favor of an interpretation of Judaism focused on social justice was presaged by my reaction to two passages in chapter 5. Amos, the earliest of the literary prophets, defined the search for the grace of God not in terms of ritual acts, not in terms of the proper practice of the sacrificial cult and ritual purity, but rather in terms of righteous living:

> *Seek good and not evil that you may live,*
> *and that Adonai, the God of Hosts, may truly be with you, as you think.*
> *Hate evil and love good,*
> *and establish justice in the gate;*
> *perhaps Adonai, the God of Hosts,*
> *will be gracious to the remnant of Joseph.* (5:14-15)

This was the positive side of Amos's formula, his conception of what God wanted of His people—goodness and justice. And then, startlingly for a Judean who knew the Jerusalem temple ritual and who was preaching at the sanctuary in Bethel,

> *I loathe, I despise your festivals;*
> *I am not appeased by your solemn assemblies.*
> *If you offer Me burnt offerings or meal offerings,*
> *I will not accept them.*
> *I will pay no heed to your gifts of fatlings.*
> *Spare Me the sound of your hymns,*
> *and let Me not hear the music of your lutes.*
> *But let justice well up as water,*
> *righteousness as an unfailing stream.* (5:21-2)

To this very day, I cannot read that last verse without feeling the reverberations of the divine voice. I hear it echoing in the chambers of my heart: "*Let justice well up as water, righteousness as a mighty stream*"—God's proclamation to the Israel of antiquity, God's proclamation to *me* today!

I pause for a moment to absorb the magnificence of that imperative and am then confronted by this startling question:

> *Did you offer sacrifice and oblation to Me*
> *those forty years in the wilderness, O House of Israel?* (5:25)

What!! The prophet, clearly familiar with the Torah tradition of the Israelites' forty years of wandering in the Sinai Desert and all of the details of the Levitical sacrificial cult, denies that sacrifices were a feature of those years? How is that possible? When I, a confused fourteen-year-old, approached Rav Riger and timidly asked him what Amos meant by that question, he answered, in line with most of the medieval commentators, that the sacrificial cult was the responsibility of the priests and Levites, not of the people, and that that was what Amos meant. I was not satisfied.

The question remained hanging for me, especially when I later found the same idea in Isaiah ("*What need have I of all your sacrifices . . . Your new moons and festivals fill Me with loathing*" 1:10-17) and in Jeremiah ("*I did not speak to your fathers nor command them . . . concerning burnt offerings and sacrifices,*" 7:21-23). Isaiah, Jeremiah, Micah, and several other prophets either condemned sacrifice as never having been ordained by God or as of lesser importance than ethical living; but Amos was the first of these. And in the case of Amos it seems quite clear that this earliest of the literary prophets, living at a time when the text of the Torah was probably not yet fixed and there was lively disagreement about the primacy of ethics or ritual, questioned whether animal sacrifice had ever been a part of God's plan for Israel. He was, in effect, denying that a major part of the Torah, a part that I myself felt was troublesome, was of God. And so it was that at the age of fourteen I added Amos to my personal list of Jewish heroes.

As courageous as Amos's denial of the essentiality of animal sacrifice would have been under any circumstances, it was doubly and triply courageous in the existential situation of that denial. First, he was in hostile territory; he was a Judean preaching in Israel. Second, he was in Bethel, the city of the sanctuary built to rival Jerusalem as the divinely chosen center for the sacrificial cult. Third, he had no credentials. What right had he, a self-described "cattle breeder and a tender of sycamore figs" (7:14), to speak? And that was precisely the question put to him after members of the mob went to the Bethel authorities to complain about Amos's heretical utterances.

The high priest of the Bethel sanctuary at the time that Amos delivered his scathing denunciation of the practices there was Amaziah. There was no way that Amaziah could allow anyone, much less an uncouth Judean ranter, to announce to a crowd that God disapproved of the fertility rites ("*Father and son go to the same girl.*") practiced at the Bethel altar and of the priests there taking wine and garments from the poor for personal use. And so he hastily sent a message to the king, Jereboam:

> *Amos is conspiring against you within the House of Israel. The country cannot endure the things he is saying. For Amos has said, "Jereboam shall die by the sword, and Israel shall be exiled from its soil." (7:10-11)*

Amaziah quite conveniently omitted Amos's harshest condemnations, against the venal and immoral practices of the priests, but he was quite accurate in accusing Amos of sedition against the royal house. There is no record of any reply that Amaziah may have received from King Jereboam, but either on his own authority or on the king's behalf, he then confronted Amos with these threatening words:

Seer, off with you to the land of Judah! Earn your living there, and
do your prophesying there. But don't ever prophesy again at
Bethel for it is a king's sanctuary and a royal palace. (12-13)

Here I must digress for a moment to explain something about prophecy
before and after the time of Amos. I have referred to Amos as the earliest of
the literary prophets. What do we mean by "the literary prophets"? Before
the time of Amos, there were several charismatic (and possibly ecstatic) seers
who are noted in particular as advisors to kings or as itinerant wonderworkers,
often the leaders of a prophetic band, who left behind no written record of
their utterances. The most noteworthy in that category were Nathan, Elijah,
and Elisha. We may refer to these and several others before the time of Amos
as nonliterary prophets.

Amos, followed quickly by Hosea and Isaiah, initiated a tradition of powerful
and often poetic oratory, spoken in the name of God. Their essential message
was that God demanded adherence to the *berit*—the covenant of justice and
righteousness that is the essence of the book of Deuteronomy. It is more
than likely that the author(s) of Deuteronomy were strongly influenced by
Amos, Hosea, Isaiah, and Micah. Amos was the prototype of this school of
God-intoxicated moral giants who established what we know as the prophetic
tradition.

Having had no experience with orators who claimed to speak in the name of
the God of Israel other than itinerant "professionals" like Elijah and Elisha who
roamed through Israel in the generations just before Amos, Amaziah looked
upon Amos as one of them. Like lepers or lunatics, they were considered to
have been "touched" by God and so while they were often threatened or even
imprisoned, they were rarely executed. And so Amaziah, in effect, told Amos
to shut up and go home.

But it was important for Amos to explain to Amaziah that he was not one
of these itinerant ecstatics who were known as *neviim* (prophets). And so,
before the frightening execration that were his parting words to Amaziah,
he explained,

I am not a prophet nor a prophet's disciple; I am a cattle breeder and a
tender of sycamore figs. But Adonai took me away from following the flock,
*and Adonai said to me: "Go, prophesy to My people Israel." * (7:14-15)

We find this dramatic confrontation, which concludes with Amos's predicting the rape of Amaziah's wife and the exile and execution of Amaziah and his sons, at the end of chapter 7, but we have to go back to chapter 3 to find the exquisite passage in which Amos explains how it is that he, the simple peasant, came to Bethel to speak in the name of God. No, he was not a professional; he was not mentored by an Elijah as Elisha was. Why did he have no choice but to deliver God's warning in Bethel? He explained as an honest farmer might, employing the vocabulary that he knew best:

> *Can two walk together without having met?*
> *Does a lion roar in the forest when he has no prey?*
> *Does a young lion cry out from its den without having made a capture?*
> *Does a bird drop on the ground, trapped, with no snare there?*
> *Does a trap spring up from the ground without having caught something?*
> *When a shofar is sounded in a town, do the people not take alarm?*
> *Can misfortune come to a town if Adonai has not caused it?*
> *Indeed, Adonai my God does nothing without having revealed His*
> *purpose to His servants, the prophets.*
> *A lion has roared, who can but fear?*
> *Adonai my God has spoken, who can but prophesy?* (3:3-8)

Arieh shaag (a lion has roared), *mi lo yiyra* (who can but fear)? Could there possibly be a person "with soul so dead" that he or she is not moved—moved thrillingly, terrifyingly—by those words? Is it only I, I whose father's name was Arieh and whose fortissimo pleas from the pulpit thrilled me while his angry reproaches terrified me, who am so shaken by those words?

Once, as a boy leaving the synagogue after my father's rendition of the Yom Kippur *Ne'ilah* service, I heard a congregant refer to him as *shaagat arieh* (the roaring of a lion) and I was so proud. That was my immediate association when I first heard that clearly reasoned cause-and-effect passage read by Rav Riger. Yes, I thrilled to that roar but I was also, too often, frightened by it. Oh yes, Amos, I have heard the roar of the lion and I was frightened, cause and effect. Yes, Amos, if God had spoken to me, I too would have faced whatever dangers there might have been and I too would have prophesied.

That was the passage that explained the phenomenon of prophecy to me. In the simple and utterly logical rhetoric of the farmer called by God, I came to understand that every effect has a cause. If two people walk together, it is because they have agreed to do so. If a trap springs, it is because it has caught something. If a tocsin is sounded, people will be alarmed. Cause and effect.

> *A lion has roared, who can but fear;*
> *Adonai has spoken, who can but prophesy.*

And thus, we the Jewish people, were given the sublime gift of Amos, Hosea, Isaiah, Micah, Jeremiah, Ezekiel . . .

Turn 14

They who go down to the sea
in ships.

—*Psalms 107:23*

I grew up in a seaside town on Boston's north shore. The sound of waves smashing relentlessly against the rocky shore about one hundred yards from my bedroom was a constant accompaniment to my dreams. We spent entire days on the beach during the hot summer months; and we felt the power of the North Atlantic, pounding wildly against the seawall and sending up spumes of chilling spray, during winter nor'easters. One of my most vivid childhood memories is of standing on the shore drive at the corner of our street clutching my father's hand and looking out at a fierce sea during the hurricane of 1938. We ran back to our house when we saw the seawall beginning to crumble and returned the next day to find a major part of the shore drive gone, simply washed out to sea.

The ocean was an ever-present reality to anyone who lived on the short sidestreets off the shore drive. Our very addresses served as constant reminders: our street was Neptune and then came Mermaid, Coral, Trident, Seafoam, Wave Way, Pearl, and Dolphin. Our telephone exchange was Ocean; our narrow gauge railroad station was Ocean Spray; and our eastward landmarks were the massive breakwaters, Graves Light and Boston Light.

My father enjoyed nothing more than a day of fishing about a mile or two beyond the breakwater in one of the gray dories rented out from the boathouse anchored offshore. When I was about seven, he took me along for the first time and taught me how to bottom fish with bloodworms. The boats that we rented had no motors, no fish finders, and, as I think back with dismay, no lifejackets. My father would simply row out to where he thought the fish might be, and we would drop our lines. More often than not, we would return with a dozen or so flounder and cod, and I would take most of them around to our neighbors as smelly but welcome gifts.

It will come as no surprise that I grew up loving everything about "our" ocean. It wasn't until a few years later that I could handle *Moby Dick*; but *Treasure Island, Robinson Crusoe,* and particularly Richard Henry Dana's *Two Years Before the Mast* were the favorite literary fare of this bibliovore in knee pants. And it was at about that time that Spencer Tracy and Freddie Bartholomew appeared in *Captains Courageous*, probably my first movie. I can still recall vividly scenes from that tale about young Harvey's evolution from spoiled brat to apprentice fisherman, guided by the patient Portuguese, Manuel. And when my parents took the family on a picnic a few miles up the coast to Gloucester and I saw the Fishermen's Memorial Monument for the first time, I read the inscription below, "*They who go down to the sea in ships*" with reverence, having no idea that it came from the Bible.

My father, of course, would never let a pedagogic opportunity slip by and so he told me where the phrase came from, and he repeated that entire verse from Psalms to me in Hebrew, "*Yordei ha-yam ba-oniyot, osei m'lacha b'mayim rabim* (They who go down to the sea in ships, they ply their trade in the mighty waters)." He instructed me to learn the verse by heart in the original and I did so quite willingly, thinking of Spencer Tracy, Richard Henry Dana, and the heroic bronze icon of Gloucester. Someday . . . someday . . .

Before proceeding, just a few words about Psalm 107. It is a hymn of thanksgiving by a person who has been "*redeemed from adversity.*" The author describes several different kinds of people and the dangers that might befall them. There are those who have lost their way in the wilderness, there are those who have been enslaved, there are those who act foolishly, and there are "*those who go down to the sea in ships.*" All ultimately come to see the redeeming power and the love of God. It is a pious psalm and for the most part, exactly what one might expect from a poet of faith. But the description of the vicissitudes of seamen is not what one might expect at all. It is the work of a poet who knew the sea, who had experienced its power, and was in awe of it. Those seven verses are absolutely magnificent:

> *They who go down to the sea in ships,*
> *who ply their trade in the mighty waters;*
> *they have seen the works of Adonai,*
> *and His wonders in the deep.*
> *By His word He raised a storm wind*
> *that made the waves surge,*

mounting up to the heavens,
plunging down to the depths.
Disgorging in their misery,
they reeled and staggered like drunken men,
all their skill to no avail.
In their adversity they cried to Adonai,
and He saved them from their troubles.
He reduced the storm to a whisper,
the waves were stilled.
They rejoiced when all was quiet,
and he brought them to their desired port.

I love the sea; my most cherished memories of an often harsh and demanding father are of those halcyon days that we spent fishing together between the Winthrop breakwater and Graves Light. He taught me to bait a hook, to feel the texture of the seafloor through my finger on the line, to distinguish between the fish that we would take home and those that we threw back, and to feel my heart leap whenever one of us cried, *Gotcha*! And so it should come as no surprise that during all the years of my education and my subsequent decades as a congregational rabbi, I longed for the day when I would own a boat and be able to go fishing whenever I wanted.

That day finally came when, at the age of sixty-six and in good health, I decided to retire from the pulpit. I had had a satisfying and I believe, productive rabbinate, but after forty years of answering to the ceaseless demands of congregants and the constant search for grist for the sermonic mill, *my* time had come. I wanted to read books for the simple joy of reading without feeling the need to mark passages for future sermons; I wanted to be able to choose partners for honest dialogue and not have to worry that Mrs. Epstein with the blue hair in the fourth row might be offended by my suggestion that Africans and Hispanics and gays were equally the children of God; I wanted to go to sleep nights without the awareness that the phone might ring with some emergency, real or imagined. I wanted to be free—*free at last, free at last*—and . . .

The closer that I came to my retirement date, the more I could smell the salt air and the fish. My wife and I love Maine in the summer; we honeymooned there and had been returning each summer for a couple of weeks, renting a variety of seaside cottages. We always chose places near boatyards where

I could rent a small outboard and test the waters off one or another of the rugged midcoast peninsulas. Then with retirement, freed from the demands of my pulpit, came the moment of truth: the time to buy a boat of my own, to *go down to the sea in*—well, not actually a ship, but at least in a boat of my own.

Within a week of my final pulpit appearance, we were off to Maine. It took us a few days to settle into a lovely little cottage on a cove off Casco Bay, and then I set off to find a boat. I worked my way back and forth along Route 1, from boatyard to boatyard, checking out Grady-Whites, Boston Whalers, Bayliners, new and used, wood and fiberglass, walkarounds, and cuddies. What I wanted was a boat with enough power and stability to take me out beyond the coves and bays to the ocean of my childhood, to twenty or thirty fathoms of blue sea where fish might be lurking below. By the third week of July, I found what I was looking for—a twenty-four-foot inboard with a small cuddy, a bait reservoir, four rod holders, and . . . *a pulpit! A pulpit!*

That's what the brochure said and that's what the boatyard owner called the two-foot extension from the bow where the anchor was secured—*a pulpit!* The boat was just what I was looking for and when the owner agreed to throw in an electronic fish finder, guaranteed to expose any unsuspecting fish swimming below, the deal was closed. With my father, it was muscle and instinct; with me, a 300-horse engine and a fish finder. And it's legal!

But a pulpit?? As soon as I returned home from the boatyard, I looked it up and there it was after the more standard definitions: "*a small railed platform at the bow of a boat.*" *Voila!* My retirement pulpit. And then I recalled that enigmatic statement by Ishmael in the eighth chapter of *Moby Dick*: "*The world's a ship on its passage out, and not a voyage complete, and the pulpit is its prow.*" The pulpit is its prow!

And so in retirement, fishing has taken on a whole new dimension. I have a seaborne pulpit where I can stand, like the savage harpooner Queequeg or Captain Ahab himself, and scan the horizon for a breaching whale. I am by no means as arrogant as King Canute commanding the waves to recede, no, I prefer to remain on friendly terms with the unpredictable sea. I have seen "*the storm wind that made the waves surge, mounting up to the heaven, plunging down to the deep.*" Having checked first with weather radio, I trust that God will still the waves and allow me to make it home.

On a slow day, I put my rod in its holder, set the drag and the clicker, and ascend my pulpit. There I stand, one hand poised to grab the rail, as I address my new congregation—a pair of curious seals, a swooping osprey, a pod of playful porpoises, or a minyan or two of gulls in the wake of a lobster boat, all *"the works of Adonai and His wonders in the deep."* I preach to the waves and unlike blue-haired Mrs. Epstein in the fourth row, they lap it up. I do let loose an occasional sermonic volley at the prickly sculpins that steal my bait and at the annoying thicket of lobster buoys with their entangling lines, but ah, the freedom! No carping critics, no gimmicky titles for the newsletter, no agonizing hours of preparation, no . . .

Suddenly a sharp *zzzzz* from the stern! I leap from my pulpit, barely missing the coiled anchor line, and grab for the quivering rod. It's a big one, maybe a striper, and the fight is on! I thrill to the arc and strain of the rod and smile toward the bow. What a magnificent new pulpit!

Turn 15

Don't I have enough lunatics?

—1 Samuel 21:16

One of the favorite words of those who like to spice their conversation with Yiddishisms is *meshuga*. This word has been so thoroughly absorbed into American English that I found it in my thesaurus along with *nutty*, *daffy*, *dotty*, *loony*, *whacky*, *balmy*, *bonkers*, *cuckoo*, and over fifty synonyms for *crazy*. But unlike all those other informal or slang locutions, *meshuga* has a rather noble provenance. It does not derive, as do so many Yiddish words, from medieval German or Polish but rather from classical Hebrew. *Meshuga*, in various forms, may be found in five different books of the Bible and in one of those books, Samuel 1, we find it repeated three times in one fascinating story.

Before going on to describe the circumstances that occasioned the use of that pungent word, I want to devote a few paragraphs to the man who first uttered it, Achish, the King of Gath. Someone should write a book or at least a monograph on the many non-Israelite characters in the Bible who interacted in a positive or even a heroic way with our patriarchs, kings, and prophets. Very prominent among these would be our Achish who on two occasions saved the life of the young David, once when he was fleeing the jealous rage of King Saul and the second time when other Philistine leaders wanted to dispose of him.

Among others in this category of benign non-Israelites would be Jethro, the priest of Midian, who took Moses into his home and then later offered him wise counsel (Exod. 2 and 20); the Tyrian king Hiram who was a devoted ally to both King David and King Solomon (2 Sam. 5 and 1 Kings 5); Ebed-Melech, the empathetic Ethiopian eunuch who saved Jeremiah's life (Jer. 38); and Naaman, the leprous commander of the army of Aram, who accepted the God of Israel after his cure by Elisha (2 Kings 5). There are others, but these in particular, fascinate me and none more so than Achish.

Not only did King Achish of Gath save David's life but while doing so in the first instance, he delivered himself of what has to be the funniest line in the entire Bible. I have caught myself mumbling that line sotto voce on numerous occasions in the course of my rabbinate, especially at congregational and organizational board meetings. I mutter that immortal line as a mantra, and it enables me to endure with relative equanimity and silence what so often has to be endured. And so I thank Achish of Gath and I bless the chroniclers who saw fit to retain his story, along with the fascinating stories of the others "Israelophiles" mentioned above. And so, what about Achish?

We are told that Achish was the king of Gath, one of the five major Philistine cities, along with Gaza, Ashkelon, Ashdod, and Ekron, that we come across in the books of Judges, Samuel 1 and 2, and Kings 1 and 2. The Philistines seem to have originated somewhere in the Aegean Sea and settled along the southwest coast of the land of Canaan around the time of Joshua. From that time on through the period of the early kings, they were a constant thorn in the side of the Israelites. Samson's heroic deeds were accomplished against the Philistines. Saul fought several battles against them and was finally defeated by them at Mount Gilboa. David became the hero of Israel by defeating the Philistine champion, Goliath of Gath. And when David wanted to marry Michal, the daughter of King Saul, the bride-price required of him was one hundred Philistine foreskins. Ever the overachiever, the young David brought back two hundred.

When the Israelites, mightily impressed by the prowess of David, began lionizing him and comparing his deeds with those of King Saul, to the latter's detriment, Saul became jealous of David. And when the common people began chanting, *"Saul has slain his thousands; David, his tens of thousands,"* Saul's jealousy turned to uncontrollable rage. He became obsessed with the need to kill David; and the story of Saul's campaign against the usurper, as he saw him, is the main substance of the last thirteen chapters of the book of Samuel 1. It is in these chapters that we first encounter King Achish.

Although the prophet Samuel had anointed David as king even before his battle with Goliath, David was then still a boy. And Saul, though he had lost the favor of God and Samuel, was still king and was determined to remain king. And so we find David fleeing attempt after attempt by Saul to kill him in those thirteen chapters, and on several occasions David is forced to flee to caves and even to the protection of Israel's enemies. It is not entirely clear why these enemies, particularly the Philistines, would have wanted to provide refuge to an Israelite hero who had not only beheaded their champion, Goliath, but also mutilated the genitalia of two hundred of them but they were probably acting in the spirit of the old adage that the enemy of my enemy is my friend. As long as David was the sworn enemy of King Saul and a pretender to his throne, the Philistines were guardedly willing to offer him protection, expecting him to become their vassal once they had disposed of Saul. And that brings us to the terse and remarkable story of David's first meeting with King Achish.

David's situation was desperate; he had lost his small band of Judean followers and even his weapons. He was reduced to lying in order to procure a sword with which to defend himself, a subterfuge that ultimately proved fatal to the priest Ahimelech who helped him (1 Sam. 21-22). Surrounded and harassed wherever he went by the agents of King Saul, David's only hope was to find refuge in one of the cities of the Philistines, and so he approached King Achish of Gath. But as soon as he was recognized, Achish's courtiers reminded the king of David's history with them. They said,

> [He's] the one of whom they sing as they dance:
> "Saul has slain his thousands;
> David, his tens of thousands."

When David realized that he was recognized and that his life was now in danger not only from Saul but from the people of Gath as well, "*he became very much afraid of King Achish of Gath.*" And so once again he resorted to a subterfuge:

> So he concealed his good sense from them; he feigned madness . . .

Now what's that all about? Why did he feign madness, to the extent of scratching marks on the gates of the city and letting saliva drip down his beard? It seems that there was a longstanding tradition among the ancients not to harm lunatics. They were in the category of "touched" by God and therefore untouchable by human beings. And so when the courtiers seized David and brought him to the king for summary execution,

> Achish said to his courtiers: "You see the man is raving; why bring him to me?"

Achish refused to order the execution of David because conventional ethics required that no one harm a lunatic. And so he told his courtiers, in effect, to shoo David out of the city.

The story would have been a memorable one if it had concluded right there, with that empathetic decision by the king. But no, he added one more statement, a remark that has me eternally in his debt, a remark, as I mentioned above, that has enabled me to maintain my equanimity and to endure what public servants must so often endure stoically. He added,

"Don't I have enough lunatics?" Don't I have enough lunatics?!!

I like it even better in Hebrew. Three simple words: *Hasar meshugaim ani?*

O Achish, how I identify with you! How much I owe you for providing me with the words that have so often accompanied my looking up toward heaven, rolling my eyes and shaking my head in disbelief.

- I raise an issue at a meeting of the congregational board: What shall we do about the lavish wedding and Bar/Bat Mitzvah receptions that create an atmosphere of excess, gluttony, and waste that is the very opposite of mitzvah? Can we, perhaps, require the hosts to contribute at least a part of their expenses to some food kitchen or shelter or perhaps to Mazon, an organization directed to the alleviation of hunger? The discussion that ensues is a positive one and I feel that I have accomplished something worthwhile until Mrs. Goldstein of the sisterhood raises her hand: "What about the rugalach that I bake for the *oneg*; are you going to tax that too?" The discussion concludes without a decision. I look up and roll my eyes. *Hasar meshugaim ani?*

- I deliver an impassioned sermon on a Yom Kippur in 1972, suggesting a national day of atonement for our sins in Vietnam. I can sense that the congregation is with me, that the awesome mood of the day has moved them to empathy with the Vietnamese and American casualties of senseless slaughter. But the mood is shattered when a congregant yells out: "A rabbi shouldn't talk politics!" *Hasar meshugaim ani?*

- At a meeting of the Federation's Political Action Committee, we discuss whether or not to react to the application of three American

Nazis to demonstrate in a nearby suburb. A police investigation has made it clear that only these three will be involved and that they are not connected to any outside hate group. We are all in agreement that a counterdemonstration would be a big mistake, that if a few hundred Jews turned out to confront three harmless cranks, the media would have a feeding frenzy. We are about to move on to other business when a man, a concentration camp survivor, yells out in a rage: "That's how Hitler started!" He is adamant, if we don't show up to confront those Nazis, we will be appeasers, like Chamberlain, and the American Nazis will grow and kill Jews! Nobody will contradict the survivor, and the committee agrees to a counterdemonstration. On the appointed day, three seedy Nazis, dozens of television cameras, and a thousand Jews, many in veterans uniforms, show up. The three brown-shirted cranks are delighted and are given camera time to vent their spleen. They and our survivor have won. *Hasar meshugaim ani?*

• After a funeral service, I am driving to the cemetery in the family limo. The three adult sons, two of their wives, and the youngish widow of the eighty-six-year-old deceased, his third wife and the primary heir to his rather large estate, are in the back. There is an oppressively heavy silence in the car until one of the sons blurts out, "I'll bet you killed him." Through her sobs, she screams, "He died of a heart attack! I loved him! He was very old!" The other two sons and the daughters-in-law join in, "You're nothing but a fortune seeker!" "Whore!" "You made him have his heart attack!" "Who've you been screwing on the side?" From the front seat, I try to calm them down. I try reason: "This is no time for a family squabble . . . Let's think about Charlie . . . We all loved him . . . This would have made him very unhappy . . . He left you all quite comfortable . . . Let's stop the bickering and bury Charlie in peace . . ." It doesn't help. The accusations, insults, and threats continue for the half hour that it takes us to reach the cemetery. I help the distraught widow stumble to the graveside. As the crowd gathers, I look heavenward, roll my eyes, and mumble, *Hasar meshugaim ani?*

• I get a phone call from a board member, a notorious gossip and snob, informing me that she heard that one of our classrooms is supposed to be named after the recently deceased father of one of our members.

Is it true? she asks. I answer in the affirmative and tell her about the substantial sum contributed by the family to the congregation for this memorial. She then blurts out, "You've got to stop it, Rabbi! This will be the first time that any room in our beautiful temple is named for an East European Jew!" *Hasar meshugaim ani?*

I know how Achish felt. He had a city to govern. He had people on all sides demanding food, water, jobs, housing, justice. He didn't have to deliver weekly sermons and deal with a confirmation class but he did have to deal with his squabbling courtiers, his harem, the rival kings of Gaza, Ashkelon, Ashdod, and Ekron, to say nothing of King Saul. He was a busy man, trying to balance the often unreasonable demands of one group against another and all of a sudden his courtiers confront him with a raving maniac, dribbling spittle down his beard and seeking asylum. I can see Achish rolling his eyes heavenward and crying out in exasperation, "*Hasar meshugaim ani!* Don't I have enough lunatics here in Gath that I have to deal with every day? You had to bring me another one?! Get out!!"

I could never bring myself to yell, "Get out!" After all, I'm a rabbi, not an oriental despot.

But thank you, Achish . . .

Or is it Abimelech? Why suddenly Abimelech?

Well, there is a strange postscript to the story of Achish and David. There is a psalm (34) that begins with the superscription:

> *Of David, when he feigned madness in the presence of Abimelech, who turned him out, and he left.*

The psalm goes on to thank God, in acrostic verses, for helping the author through difficult situations. There is no further mention of the incident in 1 Samuel 21, and one can only surmise that the author was inspired to compose this beautiful hymn of praise by the story of the hapless refugee, David, having to act like a lunatic in order to keep from being killed by the Philistines. The last verse, in particular, the only one that does not fit into the acrostic, seems a good description of the plight of David at that time:

Adonai redeems the life of His servants;
all who take refuge in Him shall not be ruined.

But the obvious question is, Who is Abimelech? Why does the superscription not read, "*When he feigned madness in the presence of Achish?*" There is no really satisfactory answer to this conundrum, but the traditional rabbinic solution is that Achish and Abimelech were the same person. Why, then, did the psalmist call him Abimelech? Because in the same way that all Egyptian kings were called Pharaoh (rather than Ramses, Thutmose, Necho, etc.,) Philistine kings were called Abimelech. It was, according to the rabbinic tradition, an apt title for a dynasty; *Abimelech* means "father of the king" or "my father is king."

Was it a scribal error? Were Philistine kings, in fact, known by the honorific Abimelech? There is some support for that theory in the fact that the king of Gerar at the time of Abraham and Isaac (see Gen. 20, 21, and 26) was also called Abimelech. And he is identified in 26:1 not only as the king of Gerar but also as the king of the Philistines. And so, Achish? Abimelech? Whatever his name, I owe him my gratitude and I dedicate this "turn" to his memory.

Turn 16

*These are the names of the sons
of Israel who came into Egypt.*

—Exodus 1:1

It is a time-honored principle of rabbinic Torah commentary that the sacred text is never repetitious. That is to say that if a phrase or a law is found in two or even three different places in the Torah, each occurrence was intended to teach something different. A conspicuous example of what might be considered repetition is the very first verse of the book of Exodus: "*These are the names of the sons of Israel who came into Egypt . . .*" It is from this verse that the Hebrew name of the book, *Shemot* (names), is derived and it is, of course, followed in the next few verses by the names of Israel's (i.e., Jacob's) twelve sons.

The problem, if indeed there is a problem, is that this very same verse may be found toward the end of Genesis: "*These are the names of the sons of Israel who came into Egypt . . .*" (46:8). In the Genesis text, these introductory words are followed by the names of the twelve sons along with the names of their sons and in some cases, their grandsons. In the opening verses of Exodus, we have first the names of the eleven sons who descended to Egypt and then the name of Joseph, but both lists include the same twelve names and conclude with the statement that there were seventy souls in Jacob's clan. And so, why this repetition?

For the dispassionate biblical scholar who does not consider every word of scripture to be unique and sacrosanct, such repetition does not constitute a problem. Some ancient scribe, setting out to tell the story of the Egyptian bondage, began with a review of the details that led to the presence and the subsequent enslavement of the Israelites in Egypt. Quite naturally, he began with a list of the ancestors who had come down to Egypt in the first place. Thus the list of the sons, repeated from the Genesis story. But for the traditionalist, there had to be a divine reason for the repetition. It had to convey something that was not implicit in the first list.

Over the centuries, many sages have offered opinions about the list that opens the book of Exodus, but every time that I come to that passage, I am reminded of the commentary that I first heard at about the age of ten from my father, a commentary that, I later learned, he derived from the writings of the great halachic authority known as the *Baal Ha-Turim* (Rabbi Jacob ben Asher, thirteenth- to fourteenth-century Toledo). The *Baal Ha-Turim* taught that this second list of names, repeated after the deaths of the twelve sons, is meant to teach us "that they didn't change their names"!! They came down to Egypt with the names listed in Genesis 46 and they kept those same Israelite names even after living most of their adult lives as members of Egyptian society.

Now why might we have thought that the sons of Jacob/Israel would change their names? Well, what was the example that their brother Joseph, the Pharaoh's deputy, had set for them? We read in Genesis 41:45 that Joseph, when he accepted his appointment as second only to the Pharaoh, took on the Egyptian name Zaphenat-Paneah. As the brothers of the Pharaoh's Egyptianized deputy, as the sons of a father who was distinguished enough to offer his blessing to the Pharaoh (47:10), as men who settled on *"the best of the land"* (47:11), one might have thought that they would signify their high standing in Egypt by acculturating, beginning with the choice of new Egyptian names. Reuben might have become Rameses, Shimon might have become Shishak, Yehudah might have become Horus, and so on and on. So why didn't they Egyptianize their names?

Again we turn to the commentary of the *Baal Ha-Turim* who points out that immediately following the list of the eleven brothers who came down to Egypt, the text reminds us that *"Joseph was already in Egypt."* Notice: the text identifies him as Joseph, his Israelite name, not as Zaphenat-Paneah. And in the very next verse, the one that recounts the death of that immigrant generation, Joseph is again identified by his Israelite name. Back to the *Baal Ha-Turim*:

> [Joseph] commanded them not to change their names. He said to them, "Even though they changed my name to Zaphenat-Paneah, you must not change your names."

Notice *"they* changed my name." According to the *Baal Ha-Turim*, Joseph would have preferred to keep his Israelite name, but *"they,"* Pharaoh's court, required that he take on an Egyptian identity, an Egyptian name, and an Egyptian wife, Asenat, the daughter of an Egyptian priest. Joseph is usually referred to in rabbinic writings as *Yoseph Ha-Tzaddik*, Joseph, the Righteous. Why was he so honored? There are three reasons: first and most obviously, because he refused the seductive wife of his employer when she pleaded with him to sleep with her (Gen. 39); second, because he reconciled himself with his brothers rather than taking vengeance on them for selling him into slavery; and third, because of his loyalty to his heritage. In what ways did he honor his heritage? In his concern for the preservation of his and his brothers' Israelite names and in his insistence that he be buried not in some magnificent pyramid befitting Pharaoh's deputy but in the land of Canaan (Gen. 50:25), alongside his father, grandfather, and great-grandfather in the cave of Machpelah.

I believe that the names bestowed upon children are the most reliable indicators of the level of acculturation of any minority group. Some of my readers may have visited the old Jewish cemetery on the island of Curacao,* the oldest Jewish burial place in the Western Hemisphere (dating back to 1659). Situated on the downwind side of a huge oil refinery with emissions of corrosive chemicals, this amazing, but unfortunately disappearing, treasury of sepulchral art on its tombstones is world renowned. But as often as I have visited that cemetery and admired the sculptures on its "precious stones," there is another aspect of that cemetery that I find even more amazing.

Among the names on over one thousand tombstones dedicated during the first two centuries of its existence, *every one of those names* is of biblical Hebrew origin. Coincidentally or not, every Jew on the island was a member of the synagogue during those years and as far as can be determined, there was no intermarriage. Toward the end of the nineteenth century, we begin to find such names as George, Oliver, and Richard. And again, coincidentally or not, intermarriage became a problem in the community at the same time. The decisions that we make about the names that our children will carry through their lives are not, I believe, decisions that we should take lightly.

All of the foregoing is but a prologue to the revelation of one of my pet peeves. I'll begin with the positive, a sentimental confession. During the

---

* Information about the old cemetery (*bet haim*) in Curacao may be found in *Precious Stones of the Jews of Curacao*, Isaac Emmanuel, 1957.

forty years of my pulpit rabbinate, there was nothing that I enjoyed more than the naming of babies. In the early years of my rabbinate, it was usually only the girls who were named in the synagogue, the boys having been named at their circumcision ceremonies. But I made it a point to encourage the parents of all the babies, male and female, born into the congregation to bring the naming ceremonies into the synagogue, reinforcing the idea of the congregation as an extended family. Not only did I enjoy those naming ceremonies, but one could tell from the "oohs" and "aahs" of the congregants that they were all *schepping nachas* along with the proud parents and grandparents.

So what's my peeve? What fault could I possibly find with so benign a ceremony, one that I admit I enjoyed? Believe me, I have no desire to offend happy parents who obviously value their Jewishness enough to bring their personal *simchahs* into the synagogue, *but* . . .

But what, dear friends, what are we saying to our beloved children when we name them after movie stars or rock musicians or soap opera characters or other flash in the pan celebrities? What message are we conveying to them when we give them specifically Scottish, Irish, or British names? And when we give the little darlings cutesy names or frivolously contrived names, what are we telling them about maturity and the sacred heritage that they will be called upon to affirm at their Bar and Bat mitzvahs, at their weddings, and in their later years as parental exemplars?

Some examples, and again I certainly intend no offense. These are simply names that I and colleagues of mine have had to affirm and bless before our congregations: Chad, Gregg, Kelsey, Kris, Sean, Darryl, Dustin, Jace, Ian, Scott, Kyle, and the like for boys; Britney, Courtney, Jaclyn, Tiffany, Tara, Chelsea, Nicole, Ashley, Christie, Farrah, Samantha, and the like for girls. There are enough Jewish children with these names today that I cannot be accused of offending the sensibilities of any particular family. (I am omitting some of the more bizarre names to which I have been exposed for fear of insulting specific families.)

"But, Rabbi," you chide me, "What's in a name? That which we call a rose by any other name would smell as sweet." Well, that may be good Shakespeare, but it's bad Judaism. Jewish tradition is full of beautiful and meaningful names. I can understand a parent not wanting to name a child Zebulun or Jezebel or Jehosaphat or Jochebed, but there are so many lovely names in our rich and ancient tradition, hundreds of strong and gentle and euphonious names. There are names with character, names that remind us that "if we ourselves are not prophets, we are the sons and daughters of prophets."

Our great-grandparents, born for the most part into communities with deep roots into our sacred tradition, had enough sense of self—of who they were and what they represented—to avoid the popular, the transitory, the current fad, and to opt for the solid, the enduring, and the true. Try these on for size: Sarah, Joshua, David, Esther, Jonathan, Deborah, Jeremy, Rachel, Zachary, Elizabeth, Adam, Joel, Daniel, and scores of other traditional names from our Bible. And by the way, for those who want to give their children "real American" names, it is these and similar biblical names that one finds so often inscribed on Revolutionary War and Civil War monuments. There were no pioneer Chads or Tiffanys or Dustins or Britneys.

I am by no means suggesting that we restrict ourselves to biblical names, although I must admit a prejudice for such names. There are dozens of other beautiful names derived from Hebrew or from Jewish history, names like Gil, Liza, Arielle, Ron, or even John and Matthew, the former derived from the Hebrew Yohanan and the latter from Mattityahu—a virtually endless treasury of names that remind a Jewish child that he or she represents a noble tradition and not some long-forgotten rock phenom.

While we are on the subject of names, indulge me as I proceed to a related peeve. I cannot count the times that new parents have come to me with such questions as, What is the Hebrew for George? or Ethel? or William? or Carol? There is no Hebrew equivalent for an Anglo-Saxon or French or Russian name. It is very likely that Grandpa George or Grandma Ethel had a Hebrew or possibly a Yiddish name and that their parents gave them English names that sounded like or shared an initial letter with their traditional names. But there is no way to discover for certain what that original name was unless there remains a *ketubah* or a tombstone that can be examined. And so the best that the rabbi can do is to suggest a Hebrew name that again sounds like or shares an initial with Grandma's or Grandpa's.

There is a Talmudic dictum that we might do well to remember when faced with the joyous opportunity of naming a child. Rabbi Eleazar ben Pedat taught, "One's name has an influence on one's life" (Tractate *Berachot*, 7b).

Turn 17

And Rachel stole her father's household idols.

—Genesis 31:19

In 1994, the Central Conference of American Rabbis demoted the matriarch, Rachel! There was no publicity, no public announcement, no explanation for this radical departure from a tradition of two millennia, but there it was on page 22 and on five other pages of the new "gender-sensitive" edition of the Reform prayer book, following the mention of the three patriarchs:

> The God of Sarah, the God of Rebekah, the God of Leah and
> the God of Rachel.

That the editors of the new Reform liturgy saw fit to append the matriarchs to the patriarchs was a step long overdue for an egalitarian religious movement. But the order in which they did so is, to say the least, puzzling. Search through the entire corpus of Talmudic and midrashic literature and you will find not one instance of the matriarchs listed in that order. Throughout the traditional literature, the matriarchs are referred to (see tractate *Nazir* 23b) as Sarah, Rebekah, Rachel, and Leah. The reason for the precedence of Sarah and Rebekah is obvious: they were the first two generations of matriarchs. But Rachel and Leah were sisters, both of them the wives of the patriarch, Jacob. Clearly, the ancient rabbis were following the lead of Jacob who preferred Rachel over Leah, even though Leah was the older and the first to marry him.

According to the well-known story in Genesis, Jacob had not intended to marry Leah and even though she produced more sons than Rachel, it was Rachel who gave birth to Joseph, Jacob's favorite, and it was Rachel who died giving birth to Benjamin. Even on his deathbed, Jacob spoke of his sorrow over the death of Rachel, though it had occurred decades earlier (see Gen. 48:7).

As if this were not enough to assure Rachel's precedence over Leah, in the closing verses of the book of Ruth, the crowd of well-wishers who hear Boaz's announcement of his impending marriage to Ruth, respond,

> *May Adonai make the woman who is coming into your house like Rachel and Leah.* (Ruth 4:11)

It was this verse that inspired the centuries-old blessing given by parents to daughters on the eve of Shabbat: "May God make you as Rachel and Leah." And so it should come as no surprise that the rabbis always referred to the matriarchs in the order: Sarah, Rebekah, Rachel, and Leah. Aware of all this, as I am sure the editors of the 1994 prayer book were, what was it that prompted them to reverse the positions of Rachel and Leah?

I believe that my rabbinic colleagues were motivated by two factors, the first political and the second theological. Politically the rabbis were responding to the increasingly vocal female constituency of the Reform movement. The women pointed out, quite correctly, that Abraham, Isaac, and Jacob were not bachelors and that, in fact, the Torah has quite a bit to say about their wives, Sarah, Rebekah, Rachel, and Leah. Even the generally misogynistic Talmudic sages used the word *imahot* (matriarchs) as a parallel to the word *avot* (patriarchs). And so, the women asked, why should a movement as outspokenly egalitarian as American Reform Judaism not mention the matriarchs alongside the patriarchs? Thus along with such "gender-sensitive" emendations as the elimination of the word *man* to represent humanity and *Lord* or *King* to represent God, the names of the matriarchs were appended to the names of the patriarchs. So far, so good. *But . . .*

But why did the editors consider it necessary to switch the places of Rachel and Leah in the listing of the matriarchs? In this, their motivation was questionable at best. Reading the Genesis stories with modern eyes and sensitivities, they saw Leah as a victim of male chauvinism. Jacob preferred the younger and more beautiful Rachel to Leah, Laban had to employ a ruse to get rid of his less desirable elder daughter, and even God "*saw that Leah was unloved*" (Gen. 29:31). And so the editors of the prayer book decided (without, I am afraid, really thinking the matter through) to right what they saw as an ancient wrong; they gave precedence to Leah over Rachel in the new gender-sensitive liturgy. The unfortunate result of this "politically correct" departure from tradition was to make it appear that the editors were unfamiliar with a venerable biblical and rabbinic tradition.

But let's give the editors the benefit of the doubt; let's suppose that their primary motivation was theological. What might have been a more spiritual reason for their demotion of Rachel than political correctness? Here we come to the crux of this essay. Rachel did something that, according to rabbinic interpretation, condemned her to an early death. Before Jacob and his family took their surreptitious leave of Laban's encampment in Paddan-Aram, Rachel stole her father's household idols, his teraphim. Jacob was unaware of Rachel's theft and so when Laban arrived at Jacob's camp after a pursuit of seven days and accused Jacob of theft, Jacob replied,

> *Anyone with whom you find your gods shall not remain alive! In the presence of our kinsmen, point out what I have of yours and take it. Jacob, of course, did not know that Rachel had stolen them.*
> (Gen. 31:32)

Jacob gave Laban permission to search his tent and the tents of his wives and his two concubines, but the teraphim were not found. They were, in fact, in Rachel's tent, but she had hidden them under the cushions on which she was sitting. And here the very earthy Torah text explains that she told her father that "*the way of women is upon me.*" Laban, of course, would not touch a menstruating woman or her trappings, "*thus he searched but could not find the teraphim.*"

One might have thought that the early rabbis would condemn Rachel for her theft of the teraphim. Is it possible that a Jewish matriarch was so devoted to the household idols with which she had grown up that she actually stole them so that she could continue to worship them in the land of Abraham, Isaac, and Jacob? For shame! But that was not the tack taken by the early commentators. They refused to believe that a matriarch might be guilty of idolatry, and so how did they explain it away? They decided that her deed was, in fact, a meritorious one; she stole her father's teraphim "in order to remove him from idolatry and sorcery" (*Midrash, Genesis Rabbah* 74:5).

Whatever her motives, though, Rashi was of the opinion that the reason for Rachel's premature death was Jacob's assurance to Laban that the thief of the *teraphim* "shall not remain alive" (*Rashi, Genesis* 31:32). My guess is that the editors of the 1994 Reform prayer book did not accept the midrashic explanation of Rachel's theft, that they took the text at face value and came to the conclusion that Rachel could not abandon the idolatry of her youth, that she stole the *teraphim* for the protection that they might provide in a strange new land and that she therefore, as Rashi suggests, deserved her early demise. And so, whether in the service of political correctness or in the service of pure monotheism, the editors of the 1994 prayer book demoted Rachel—wrongly, I believe.

Was Rachel really an idolatress? To answer that question properly, we must first ask another: What are teraphim? What were these so-called household gods that Rachel stole from her father? If they were simply idols, then why didn't the Torah text use the standard biblical locution for idols, *pesilim* (sing. *pesel*)? There is a curious ambiguity among the biblical authors about the nature of teraphim. It seems most likely that they were the Israelite equivalent of the considerably later Roman *lares* and *penates*, small images that were kept in homes as familial cult objects.

In at least three instances, Israelite prophets spoke disparagingly of practices involving teraphim (Ez. 21:26, Hos. 3:4, Zech. 10:2). But elsewhere in the Bible, we find at least two mentions of teraphim that seem not to be derogatory or even pagan. Michal, the daughter of King Saul and the wife of King David, had teraphim in her home and used one of them in a ruse to save David's life (1 Sam. 19:13-16). And there is a very curious story in the final chapters of the book of Judges that tells of a Levite who acted as priest for an Ephraimite family and for a troop of Danite soldiers; among the tools of his trade were teraphim. In neither of these cases is there a word of disapproval about their use. (But the seventeenth-century biblical commentator, Yehiel Hillel Altshuler, known as *Metzudat Zion*, thought it necessary to explain away Michal's connection with teraphim by explaining, "Women used to make *teraphim* in the images of their husbands so that they could gaze upon them with great love.")

It seems clear that teraphim were in common use among Israelites through most of the biblical period and that while devotion to them might have been a departure from the pure worship of Adonai, that devotion was not as sinful and execrable as idol worship. There are long tirades of condemnation in the prophetic books and in the Psalms against the worship of other gods and the adoration of *pesilim* and *elilim* (idols), but the teraphim were, for the most part, ignored. And so we return to Rachel. Was her retention of her father's teraphim a serious failure on the part of a matriarch, a grievous sin that condemned her to an early grave? I think not.

I would like to suggest that all of us carry along with us, when we leave the homes of our parents, a variety of fetishes, beliefs, and practices that may be classified as teraphim. They may be superstitions, they may be deep-seated habits, they may be "security blankets" of one kind or another, but I would hesitate to brand them as idolatry. Idolatry involves raising something up to the level of ultimate adoration—power, money, position, beauty. When these become the be-all and end-all of a person's values, that is idolatry. The veneration of teraphim, of familiar habits, beliefs, and fetishes, may be insidious and unworthy, but it does not reach the sinful level of idolatry.

I think back to one of the most liberating moments on my personal road to maturity. As a college freshman, I took a basic sociology course with a brilliant scholar, Talcott Parsons. One day, Parsons suddenly asked the class, "How many of you believe that your family doctor is the best doctor in your town?" Virtually all the students, myself included, raised hands. He looked around the room and smiled and then he explained the obvious, that all of our families could not have enjoyed the ministrations of the "best doctor" and that it was a matter of pride, if not accuracy, to most people that their families lived by the highest standards.

It took me many years to free myself from a whole series of religious fetishes that I was raised to believe were sacred but which were, in fact, teraphim. Religious communities, in particular, are susceptible to irrational customs and practices, often raising them to the status of the sacred. A few examples from our own allegedly iconoclastic religion:

- To study Torah, to teach Torah, and to live by such Torah ideals as respect for the rights of neighbors and strangers is sacred; but to *kiss* the Torah when it passes in procession in the synagogue? How is this any different from the Byzantine custom of kissing icons? *Teraphim!*

- To revere the memories of departed parents and grandparents and teachers and to attempt to live in accordance with what was noblest in them is sacred, but to believe in and pray for the imminent resurrection of a rebbe or a baba and to make a shrine of a grave?

How is this any different from circling the *Kaabah* or washing in the Ganges or venerating the femur of a saint? *Teraphim!*

- To mark one's home with a mezuzah to indicate that the occupants believe in and live by a divine code of ethics and to be aware of the meaning of that mezuzah upon entering or leaving the home is sacred, but to make a fetish of that symbol by kissing it and checking it to make sure that every letter in it is perfect is to identify with those Israeli zealots who declared that the twenty-one children of Maalot who were killed in the PLO massacre of 1974 came from homes where the mezuzot were not "kosher." *Teraphim!*

- To recall the glories of the ancient Temple in Jerusalem where people brought the offerings of their fields and prayed for the day when "God's house" would serve as "a house of prayer for all people" might stimulate the modern worshiper to sacred acts of atonement and tzedakah, but to pray today for a return to the bloody ancient Israelite sacrificial cult, as described in the Orthodox *Mussaf* service, and for the reestablishment of the hierarchical priesthood is to revert to most primitive level of Jewish worship. *Teraphim!*

- To adopt a dietary regimen that takes into consideration the humane treatment of animals, just compensation for farm laborers, moderation, gratitude, and the needs of the hungry is to live in accordance with the sacred essence of *kashrut*, but to make a fetish of *kashrut*, trying always to exceed and disdain the dietary practices of others, is to pervert the teachings of Torah. *Teraphim!*

- To make the Sabbath a day of rest, reflection, study, prayer, and joy is to create a sacred temple of time and space, but to encumber it with restriction upon restriction, including such legal fictions as stringing a wire from telephone pole to telephone pole around a neighborhood (an *eruv*) so as to allow the carrying of a handkerchief or a medication is pietistic nonsense. *Teraphim!*

There is so much excess baggage in much of today's religiosity—Jewish, Christian, Islamic, and Eastern. I am loath to reflect on religions other than my own because I have learned that the person who loves a particular religion might best correct that which is less than godly in his or her own religion before presuming to correct someone else's religion. They all contain teraphim, some more, some less.

And so we should not be surprised to read that Rachel could not resist carrying away with her the household idols, those familiar teraphim, with which she grew up. That was not idolatry; it was not a sin worthy of premature death. It was a matter of "when she grows up, she'll know better." Obviously, she did grow up; she matured to the extent that the prophet Jeremiah chose her to personify the anguish of Jewish history at the exile of the Jerusalemites.

> *Thus said Adonai:*
> *A cry is heard in Ramah, wailing and bitter weeping,*
> *Rachel weeping for her children.*
> *She refuses to be comforted for her children who are gone.*
> *Thus said Adonai:*
> *Refrain your voice from weeping, your eyes from shedding tears . . .*
> *Your children shall return to their land.* (Jer. 31:15-17)

And in 2007, with its new Reform prayer book, *Mishkan T'filah*, the Central Conference of American Rabbis saw fit to return Rachel to *her* land, to her original status among the matriarchs. That familiar rubric now reads,

> *Elohei Sarah, Elohei Rivka, Elohei Rachel, v'Elohei Leah.*

Turn 18

The righteous one (tzaddik)
shall live by his faith.

—Habakkuk 2:4

The primary purpose of the Bible is to teach righteousness. The words *tzaddik* (a righteous person); *tzedek* (righteousness); *tzedakah* (a righteous deed); and *tzadak* (the verb form in all its conjugations, indicating righteous action) occur over five hundred times and may be found in every book of the Bible. Clearly, the God of Moses, of the psalmist, and of the prophets desired that we live by the standards of *tzedek*. And if we do so, then we may join that company of whom the psalmist sang, "*Adonai ohev tzaddikim* (Adonai loves the righteous)." And so it is surely remarkable that in the entire Bible, with its dozens of stories of spiritual giants, there is only one person who is unequivocally labeled a *tzaddik*.

The patriarchs and matriarchs? Moses? Miriam? Aaron? Deborah? David? The prophets? Ruth? Mordecai? Esther? All of these heroic characters were practitioners of tzedek or tzedakah. All of them were virtuous. Abraham, in fact, was described by Isaiah as God's "beloved" (Isa. 41:8); Moses was the faithful servant of the God whom he knew "face to face" (Deut. 34:10); Ruth's loyalty earned her a "complete reward from Adonai" (Ruth 2:12); and Job was "blameless and upright" (Job 1:1). But there is only one biblical character about whom we read that he was a "*tzaddik*, blameless in his generation" (Gen. 6:9). There was only one to whom God said, "You only have I seen as *tzaddik* before Me" (7:1). And that one, as you have probably realized by now, is Noah.

What, then, was the uniqueness of Noah? Why was he singled out for that rare and ultimate biblical encomium rather than one of those others who are venerated by Jewish tradition as paragons of righteousness? As we attempt to answer those questions, we shall see the emergence of a peculiar and startling motif that one might consider almost heretical in Judaism, a motif that originates with the saga of Noah and is confirmed a few chapters later by its contrast to the career of the patriarch, Abraham.

To avoid misunderstanding, we should make mention of a few biblical instances where the title of *tzaddik* might seem to have been earned by someone other than Noah. There are a few individuals who are referred to as *tzaddikim* in the sense that they are innocent victims. Possibly the best example would be King Saul's hapless son, Ish-Boshet. After his assassination, King David referred to him as an *ish tzaddik* (2 Sam. 4:11) in the sense that he was not guilty of any offense; he was a minor character, blameless, and not deserving of death. And there is at least one other instance of this kind of usage. Saul admitted to David, "*Tzaddik ata mimeni* (You are more righteous than I)" (1 Sam. 24:18). Saul was not calling David a *tzaddik* but rather indicating that, in their dynastic struggle, it was David whose behavior was more proper.

The word *tzaddik* is also used in the Bible to refer to a category of people who are innocent of wrongdoing—examples: "They sell the *tzaddik* for silver" (Amos 2:6); "Will you destroy the *tzaddik* along with the evil person?" (Gen. 8:23); "The *tzaddik* lives by his faith" (Hab. 2:4). In none of these instances is the reference to a particular person.

There is, however, one instance where the word *tzaddik* does, in fact, refer to an individual other than Noah. Job, who is introduced as "blameless and upright," refers to himself twice as a *tzaddik*: "The innocent *tzaddik* is made a laughing-stock" (12:4) and "the *tzaddik* holds to his way" (17:9). Whereas it is the Torah narrative that describes Noah as a *tzaddik*, this unique encomium is conferred by Job on *himself*. His claim is denied by his three hypocritical "comforters" who conclude their pietistic moralizing with the words, "He is a *tzaddik* in his own eyes" (32:1). But while the three moralists might have had their own axes to grind in their refusal to accept Job's claim to the title *tzaddik*, we can impugn no such motives to God who rebukes Job for his hubris, asking, "Would you condemn Me that you might be right?" (40:8). The final two Hebrew words of that rebuke are *l'maan titzdak*, which can be translated as "so that you might be a *tzaddik*." All of this confirms God's statement to Noah: "*You only have I seen as tzaddik before Me.*"

The authentic *tzaddik* does not seek to justify or aggrandize himself. The prophet Habakkuk summed it up quite succinctly, saying, "The *tzaddik* lives by his faith." And while the final word of that statement, *emunato*, may not mean faith in the way that we define it today (i.e., religious faith, belief in God), what the prophet seems to have had in mind was steadfastness, reliability, and modesty; the *tzaddik* will endure even if he is made to suffer for his adherence to the principles of morality. Such a person was Noah in his generation. But what of Abraham?

Biblical tradition identifies Noah as the pre-Hebrew father of all humanity in contrast to Abraham, the father of the Hebrew people. Not only are Noah and Abraham identified as *physical* progenitors, but they are identified also as *spiritual* progenitors. Abraham, either by himself or in tandem with the other patriarchs and matriarchs, is invoked regularly in Jewish liturgy as the source of the *Jewish* mission, whereas Noah is invoked as the source of *universal* law. Jewish tradition posits seven commandments that are the responsibility of every human being, if he or she is to find favor with God. These seven commandments are known as "*sheva mitzvot b'nei Noah* (the seven commandments of the descendants of Noah) (Talmud, *Sanhedrin* 56a-b, *et al.*).

One can only express amazement at the fact that the Jewish tradition, which clearly prefers Abraham over Noah, reserves the title *tzaddik* for Noah. What was it about the stories of these two "founding fathers" that impelled Jewish tradition to identify the *universal* progenitor as a *tzaddik* and its own *particular* progenitor as God's beloved, as a practitioner of *tzedakah*, but not as a *tzaddik*? The solution to this conundrum may, I believe, be found in a close reading of the relevant Genesis text.

The word *tzaddik*, as we have seen, is used twice to describe Noah and not at all for Abraham. The closest that Abraham comes to meriting that unique encomium is the verse, "*Because he put his trust in Adonai, He reckoned it as tzedakah*" (15:6), usually translated as merit or righteousness. A bit further on in the Abrahamitic saga, just before the heroic plea by Abraham for the people of Sodom and Gomorrah, God says, "*I have singled him out, that he may instruct his children and his posterity to keep the way of Adonai by doing tzedakah u-mishpat*," the final two words usually translated as "righteousness and justice" (18:19).

Clearly, Abraham was a practitioner of *tzedek* or *tzedakah*, but nowhere in the Bible is he or are any of his descendants identified as *tzaddikim*. There seems to be a distinction between one who acts righteously and one who is unambiguously labeled a *tzaddik*. Rabbinic tradition is clearly bothered by the fact that Noah, not only a non- or pre-Jew but a drunkard as well

(9:18-21) is the one and only *tzaddik*. The classic rabbinic commentators focus on one word in the verse that introduces Noah that seems to modify his "*tzaddik*-hood." The text describes him as "*tzaddik b'dorotav* (in his generation)." Following the lead of Rabbi Jochanan in the Talmud (*Sanhedrin* 108a), the sages say, in effect, "Aha, he was a *tzaddik* only in his wicked generation." As the prime commentator, Rashi, put it: "By the standards of his generation, Noah was a *tzaddik*, but if he had lived in the generation of Abraham, he would have amounted to nothing" (Rashi on *Genesis* 6:9).

Rashi then goes on to buttress his anti-Noah, pro-Abraham polemic by comparing two phrases that describe the relationship between these two heroes and God. Commenting on the final words of Noah's introductory verse, "*Noah walked with God*," Rashi wrote, "But in the case of Abraham the text reads, '*Adonai before whom I walked*' (24:40). Noah needed God's close support, but Abraham was strong enough to walk by himself in his righteousness." A variation on the same theme may be found in the midrashic commentary to the same verse:

> *Noah walked with God*—Rabbi Judah said, "This may be compared to a king who has two sons, one grown up and the other a child. To the child he says, 'Walk *with* me,' but to the adult he says, 'Walk *before* me.' Similarly, to Abraham whose strength was great, he said, 'Walk *before* Me,' but to Noah who was weak, the text reads, 'Noah walked *with* God.'" (*Genesis Rabbah* 30:10)

It might seem that the sages were grasping at semantic straws in their efforts to diminish the universal Noah in behalf of the Hebrew Abraham, but they found additional support in the words used by the patriarch Jacob in his prologue to the blessing of Joseph's sons: "*The God before whom my fathers Abraham and Isaac walked*" (48:15), reminding us again that Noah is described as walking *with*, but not before, God.

Why this great effort by the Jewish sages to magnify Abraham's reputation at the expense of Noah? Here we come to the crux of the matter. There was something about Abraham's career that was in keeping with the prophetic mission of Israel, i.e., to be "*a light to the nations*," and that something was noticeably lacking in Noah. Let's compare the reactions of these two progenitors to the news of God's intention to annihilate populations—in

Noah's case, all humanity except for his immediate family, and in Abraham's case, the people of Sodom and Gomorrah.

It is Abraham who exhibits the type of behavior that the Jewish tradition generally associates with *tzedek*, faith even unto death (18:30, 32). Abraham had the courage to stand in the breech, confronting God Himself with his demand that the Judge of the entire world practice justice (18:25). Abraham, God's "beloved," argued with God; he refused to accept the decree of God without some explanation. Moses, "the servant of God," exhibited the same type of activism, of attempting to manipulate the will of God for the sake of human survival. Like Abraham, he argued with God (Exod. 32:9-14; Num. 14:11-20; and Deut. 9:12-19).

How, by contrast, did Noah, the *tzaddik*, react when informed that God intended to destroy humanity? God says, "*I will blot out man whom I have created from the face of the earth*" (6:7). Noah's reaction? Silence. God says, "*The end of all flesh is come before Me, for the earth is filled with violence*" (6:13). Noah's reaction? Silence. God says, "*I am about to bring a flood of waters upon the earth to destroy all flesh under the sky in which there is breath of life; everything on earth shall perish*" (6:17). Noah's reaction? Silence. And after God tells Noah all that he must do to save himself and his family and two (or seven) of every living creature, twice the text says, "*And Noah did everything that God commanded him to do*" (6:22 and 7:5)—in silence!

Is this the behavior of a *tzaddik*? He does not even ask God if there might be just a few decent people who deserved to be saved? After the heinous sin of the golden calf, when God informed Moses of his intention to destroy the Israelites and to make Moses into a great nation in their stead, Moses implored God to reconsider and to spare the people, and God relented (Exod. 32:10-14). Moses followed the Abrahamitic model, confirming what we might call the subsequent Jewish model of protest in behalf of humanity. But Noah? Silence.

And it is precisely this silence which, I would argue, is the essence of "*tzaddik-hood.*" Not only is Noah the only person identified as a *tzaddik*, but he is, not coincidentally, the only major character in the entire Bible who, throughout his entire interaction with God, throughout the entire episode of human destruction, never speaks! He does seemingly speak out at the very end of his story, but that concluding episode is quite separate from the essential Noah saga and according to many Bible critics (*viz.* Robert Pfeiffer and others), the story of Noah's drunkenness and nakedness is from a different hand than the flood story in which Noah does not utter one word.

For those who prefer to read the entire Noah saga, including the final verses of chapter 9, as one divine composition, what is it that could finally have moved Noah to cry out after his silence in the face of the destruction of humanity? According to the text, Noah's first act on emerging from the ark with his family was to plant a vineyard. When the grapes were ripe, he made wine and drank until he fell into a drunken stupor and stripped naked. His son Ham, as the translations delicately put it, "*saw his father's nakedness.*" What happened when Noah awoke? For the first and only time, he spoke out, cursing Ham's son, Canaan, and then, to round out that brief episode, he blessed his other two sons, Shem and Japheth, who had avoided looking on their father's nakedness.

The Talmudic sages certainly noticed that Noah did not speak during the entire flood story, and so they had to offer some explanation for his finally breaking his silence. *Ervah*, the word used in the Genesis text to describe the situation of the drunken Noah, means something far more serious than nakedness, they opined. The sin of Ham was that he castrated his father and sexually abused him!! *Ervah*, the sages suggested, is a euphemism for homosexual rape! (For that entire amazing discussion, see tractate *Sanhedrin* 70a).

According to this Talmudic tradition—supported by the Canaanite myth that tells of how the god, El-Kronos, emasculated his father and a Hurrian myth that tells of how Kumarbis severed the genitals of his father, the god Anu—the crime of Ham was so great and the indignity to Noah was so overwhelming that he spoke for the first time. In his final days, after the supreme episode of his life, the *tzaddik* Noah ceased to be a *tzaddik* because he was so totally degraded. Noah spoke out only this once, and in doing so, he ceased to be a *tzaddik*. And in the very next verses, he died.

And so how do we explain the silence of Noah through the entirety of the flood story? Why did he not cry out, as did the later Hebrew heroes Abraham and Moses, in an attempt to invoke God's mercy? Why? Precisely because he was a *tzaddik*, and the essence of the *tzaddik* is to accept the divine decree, whatever it might be, in silence. The *tzaddik* does not argue with God; he does not attempt to dissuade God from His purposes, which, he believes, are beyond human comprehension. He accepts the will of God and, if need be, he suffers with God. The *tzaddik* does not demand explanations; his unquestioning faith is the purpose of his life.

This, though, is not the Jewish model. The overwhelming weight of Jewish tradition recommends the model of Abraham who, in the name of humanity and justice, as he understood those ultimate values, confronted and questioned God. But that same Jewish tradition supplies a second model, that of Noah, the progenitor of all humanity. Noah is the father of the quietistic tradition, a tradition that can more readily be found in Christianity and certain eastern religions. Does it occur anywhere in Jewish literature other than the Noah story? Yes, there are quite a few examples in Jewish mystical texts and in Hassidic folklore, as we shall see elsewhere.* But silence is not the normative Jewish response to human suffering. The Jew is taught to be a pursuer of *tzedek*, and that pursuit may even require the chutzpah to question God. The tzaddik, though, does not question; he is content to separate himself from the human condition and to "live by his faith."

---

*   For some startling examples of silent complicity by the *tzaddik* with the will of God in Jewish literature, see Turn 19.

Turn 19

The tzaddik is the foundation of the world.

—Proverbs 10:25

We have written above about the one and only *tzaddik* in the Bible, Noah, and that it was, mirabile dictu, his silence in the face of catastrophe that marked him as a *tzaddik*. This lack of response to the annihilation of human beings seems to be the very antithesis of the biblical ideal of the pursuit of justice. Abraham conceived of God as the judge of all the world who always acts justly. And when he feared that God was not acting justly, he demanded to know why (Gen. 18:23ff). Moses sought to dissuade God when he was told that God intended to wipe out the Israelites (Exod. 32:10-14). The psalmist over and over again appeals to God to have mercy, to cure, and to redeem His people from suffering or defeat. This is the Abrahamitic model: crying out to God in the attempt to avert evil.

Abraham and Moses, along with many other heroes of Jewish scripture, were certainly practitioners of *tzedek* (righteousness), but the Bible never refers to any of them by the title *tzaddik*. That sobriquet is reserved uniquely for Noah and, as we have seen in the previous essay, Noah is also unique in that he is the only major character in the Bible who never speaks. This combination of silence and "*tzaddik*-hood" gave rise to a literary genre that can be found in early rabbinic writings and that came to full flower centuries later in Hassidic folklore.

An early midrash (*Mechilta, Shira* 1 and *Genesis Rabbah* 30:1), taking Noah as exemplar, teaches that it is only by virtue of *tzaddikim* that the world survives. There is a lengthy discussion in the Talmud (*Yoma* 38b) that also emphasizes the essentiality of the *tzaddik* for the perpetuation of humanity. Rabbi Eleazar said, "For the sake of a single *tzaddik* was this world created." And following on the heals of that statement, Rabbi Hiyya bar Abba added, "Even for the sake of a single *tzaddik* the world endures." His proof text? "The *tzaddik* is the foundation of the world" (Prov. 10:25).

Before returning to our main theme, the essential silence of the *tzaddik*, I want to devote a few paragraphs to the Talmudic discussions of the numbers of *tzaddikim* that God creates in order for the survival of each generation. In the passage from the tractate *Yoma* quoted above, Rabbi Hiyya in the name of Rabbi Johanan declared, "No *tzaddik departs from this world before another tzaddik like him is created . . . God saw that tzaddikim were rare, and so he planted them in every generation.*"

Following the lead of the late Israeli folklorist, Ephraim Urbach (*The Sages: Their Concepts and Beliefs*, Jerusalem, 1975), we can trace the development of the popular belief that God creates *tzaddikim* in every generation for whose sake that world survives. In the Talmudic tractate *Hullin* (92a), we read that "*there are forty-five tzaddikim for whose sake the world exists.*" The idea that a certain number of *tzaddikim* are essential for the survival of the world was the accepted view of the rabbis until the fourth-century Babylonian sage, Abbaye, established the number that would from then on remain a constant in Jewish folklore.

Abbaye taught, "*The world never lacks thirty-six tzaddikim who greet the presence of the Shechina in each generation.*" As his proof text for the number thirty-six, Abbaye offered a quotation from the prophet Isaiah, "*Happy are they who wait for Him*" (30:18). In Hebrew numerology, the word *lo* (for Him) is the equivalent of thirty-six. But although Abbaye chose a biblical verse to support his choice of that number, it is more likely that his source was an ancient Egyptian tradition that thirty-six *decani* (celestial beings) rule the heavens. Building on this tradition, the author of the mystical *Tikkunei Zohar* (thirteenth century?) opined, "There are thirty-six *tzaddikim* in the land of Israel and thirty-six in the diaspora."

In Hebrew numerology, thirty-six is designated as *lamed-vav*, and in the Hassidic literature from the early eighteenth century on, the tradition of the *lamed-vav* is as firmly set as Sinai. Hassidic folklore often makes a distinction between the incognito, silent *tzaddikim*, i.e., *nistarim* (hidden) and revealed *tzaddikim*, i.e., *mefursamim*, who are identifiable and are not silent. Nowhere is this more explicit than in a story retold by Elie Wiesel about the founder of Hassidism, Rabbi Elijah, the *Baal Shem Tov*, in his *Souls on Fire* (New York, 1972; p. 23):

One day [the Baal Shem Tov] sent his disciples to a village to meet a *Lamed Vavnik*, a Just Man [i.e., *tzaddik*], one of the thirty-six without whom the world could not survive. The Baal Shem Tov told the disciples: "This man resembles me like a brother; we are of the same age, we share the same origins, the same virtues and the same knowledge. Before coming down to earth, we decided jointly that we would, at the very first opportunity, observe the first commandment: that of *Kibud em*, to honor our mothers. How? We would not cry, so as not to worry them. We kept our word. I never cried in my mother's presence, though as soon as she left the house to go to market or services, I could not hold back my tears. When the neighbors remarked on her apparent insensitivity, she naturally could not understand, and naturally she suffered. As for my friend, he controlled himself even when his mother was away. And that is why it was decided above that as a reward he would be allowed to remain a hidden Just Man [i.e., a *tzaddik nistar*], whereas I was condemned to fame.

Notice two essential elements in this Hassidic tale. First, there are *tzaddikim* like the Baal Shem Tov whose righteousness is manifest, who live up to the standards of *tzedek* like Abraham and Moses while there are other *tzaddikim* who are hidden. Although Hassidic folklore refers to both the *nistarim* (the hidden) and the *mefursamim* (the revealed) as *tzaddikim*, it is the former who are the thirty-six. And the second element: the requirement of silence. The *tzaddik nistar* or *lamed-vavnik* must be unrecognized and, like Noah, silent.

There are numerous stories in the Talmud and in *aggadic* (early rabbinic folkloristic literature) compilations that are prototypes of the Hassidic *tzaddik* stories. A few examples: in the Talmud, tractate *Taanit* 22a, there is a very quaint story about a sage who happens to meet Elijah (the ubiquitous and miraculous messenger of God) in a Babylonian marketplace. The sage asks Elijah if there is anyone of particular merit in the area. At first, Elijah answers in the negative, but then a man walks in, dressed as a non-Jew, and Elijah points him out as especially meritorious. The sage approaches the man and asks him about himself. He responds that he is a jailer, and that he makes it a point, even at the risk of his life, to protect the women prisoners from the men. Asked further why he dresses as a non-Jew, i.e., why he prefers not to be recognized, he replies that as a non-Jew he often overhears plots against the Jewish community and can warn the rabbis so that they can pray and avert the menace.

A similar Talmudic story (J *Taanit* 1:4) is told about a simple donkey driver who, the rabbis discover, has the power to cause rain to fall. They ask him if he has ever done anything of particular merit. He answers,

> Once I rented a donkey to a woman who began to weep on the road. I asked her why she wept, and she told me that her husband was in prison and that she was going to the city to sell her chastity to obtain his ransom. When we came to the city, I sold my donkey and gave her the money that I received. And I said to her, "Take this and free your husband, but do not sin." The rabbis said to him, "You are indeed worthy to pray for us and be answered."

This "hidden saint" motif continues in the Zohar where we find an account of a journey undertaken by two great sages. An anonymous third man joins them to take care of the baggage and the donkeys. The sages, of course, begin discussing Torah and, as they are discussing a particularly abstruse point, the donkey driver suddenly interrupts with a complex question. The sages are unable to answer, and the stranger then launches into an erudite discourse that amazes the sages. Then,

> Rabbi Eleazar and Rabbi Abba went up to the stranger and kissed him. They said, "With all this profound knowledge that you have, is it proper that you travel behind us? Who are you?" He answered, "Do not ask my name, but let us continue to travel together and discuss Torah."

Of course, the two rabbis want to know how such a learned scholar became a donkey driver, and he gives them a contrived story that reveals nothing. When they press him further, he stops them with the information that he must hide his wisdom and fame until the coming of the Messiah (*Zohar* I: 5a-7b).

Notice the allusion to the need of this donkey driver to maintain his incognito status until the end of days. There is something in the divine scheme of things that makes it necessary for this donkey driver to remain hidden (*nistar*). Of course, in this particular story and in the two that precede it, the incognito righteous man is not silent, but he is hidden. He is silent about his essence. There are hundreds of such stories in Jewish folklore—ancient, medieval, and modern. They tell of an obscure shoemaker here, a donkey driver there, a shepherd or a water carrier somewhere else, each of who emerges from obscurity to perform a miracle, to teach a great lesson, or to avert a catastrophe. Then usually after they disappear, one or another meritorious character realizes that he has been in the presence of one about whom scripture says, *"The tzaddik is the foundation of the world."*

It is worth pointing out, having again quoted that verse from Proverbs, that there is a curious discussion in the Talmud (tractate *Hagigah* 12b) among several sages about a statement in the Mishnah by Rabbi Jose. Rabbi Jose taught that the earth is founded on pillars, and he goes on to explain that these pillars are the waters, the mountains, the winds, the storm, and the arm of God for each of which he offers biblical proof texts. It is not this mystical lesson of Rabbi Jose's that I find of particular interest but rather what follows it. Other Mishnaic sages then proceed to discuss just how many pillars are necessary to support the world. Some say twelve and offer appropriate proof texts, some say seven and quote other texts, but then along comes the second-century sage, Rabbi Eleazar ben Shamua, who declares,

> *[The world] rests on one pillar, and its name is tzaddik, as it says: "The tzaddik is the foundation of the world."*

What, then, is the function of the *tzaddik*? If, like Noah, he must accept the will of God in silence, never making any demands either for himself or for his generation, what is his raison d'etre? There is yet one more element to this puzzle that should be mentioned before we hazard an answer to that question. We have indicated that Noah is the only person in the Bible identified unequivocally as a *tzaddik*. The only *person*, yes, the only *personality*, no. God is the only other entity in the Bible who is referred to, over and over again, as *tzaddik*. A few examples:

> *A faithful God, never false; tzaddik and upright is He.* (Deut. 32:4)

> *Adonai in her midst is tzaddik; he does no wrong.* (Zeph. 3:5)

> *Adonai is tzaddik in all His ways and faithful in all His works.* (Ps. 145:17)

There are many such references to God in the Bible which makes it all the more puzzling that only Noah, seemingly unconcerned about the fate of humanity, shares this unique honorific. What can we say about this nexus, God and Noah? What about those others who are identified in postbiblical Jewish folklore as *tzaddikim* or *nistarim* or as *lamed-vavniks*? What is the function of the *tzaddik*? And if, indeed, he has some special relationship to God, why does he not use it? Why did Noah not object to the destruction of all humanity? If, as Jewish folklore suggests, there are hidden *tzaddikim* in every generation, where was the *tzaddik*, divine or human, who might have cried out and averted the Shoah?

Can a *tzaddik* revive a dead person, à la Elisha or Jesus? Can a *tzaddik* cause rain to fall? Or cure the cancer of a young mother? Or divert a speeding car about to hit a child? According to that genre of Jewish folklore that we have been quoting, the answer would seem to be yes. We find very definite corroboration for this view in the Talmudic tractate *Moed Katan* (16b) where God is astonishingly portrayed as saying, "*I rule over humankind. Who rules over Me? The tzaddik, for I make a decree and he causes me to annul it.*" The *tzaddik*, it would seem, has that power, but he does not use it. He acquiesces silently to the will of God.

There is a popular story that was artfully retold by Y. L. Peretz in the nineteenth century and can be found in most anthologies of Jewish literature. The story tells about the death of a poor and simple man, Bontsha. "In silence he was born; in silence he lived; and in silence he died." His life was a never-ending misery and he never complained.

> He was silent in that awful moment just before he was about to die, and he was silent in that very moment when he did die. And never one word of protest against man, never one murmur of protest against God.

As the story draws to its conclusion, where Bontsha is praised for his stolid faith by the heavenly court, God tells Bontsha:

> You never understood that you need not have been silent, that you could have cried out and that your outcries would have brought down the world itself and ended it. You never understood your sleeping strength.

Where did Peretz, or the generations of storytellers who transmitted this old folktale to him, find the chutzpah to suggest that a certain type of human being, by crying out, protesting, objecting, cajoling, or even praying, might upset the natural order and destroy the world? And we find a similar suggestion in the folklore surrounding the life of the eighteenth-century Rabbi Nahman of Bratzlav. Arthur Green, in his masterly biography, relates, "[Nahman] spoke of a still, small voice he possessed with which he could cry out in such a way that it would ring from one end of the earth to the other." (*Tormented Master*, New York, 1981, p. 32). But like Noah, like Bontsha, Rabbi Nahman did not use that voice. Why?

The closest that we might come to a solution of this centuries-old dilemma may be found in a well-known *piyyut* (a poetic addition to the liturgy), the theme of which originated in early medieval times and has been a part of Jewish liturgy since around the tenth century. On Yom Kippur afternoon in traditional Ashkenazic synagogues, the congregation reads *Eleh Ezkerah*, a *piyyut* that relates (unhistorically) the martyrdom of ten great sages of the second century at the hands of the Romans.

Among the ten martyrs of the *piyyut* is Rabbi Ishmael, the high priest, who was noted not only for his piety but for his physical beauty as well. The daughter of the Roman governor, seeing Rabbi Ishmael, falls in love with him and begs her father to spare him. The governor responds by ordering that the skin be flayed from his face. When this torture reaches his forehead, the place for his phylactery (*tefillin*), Rabbi Ishmael cries out bitterly. The angels take up Rabbi Ishmael's cry, challenging God: "Is this, then, the reward for a life of Torah?" And a heavenly voice answers, "If I hear another exclamation, I will instantly turn the world to water; I will return the world to primal chaos. This is my decree! Submit to it."

Why does God warn the angels to be silent? Why was the Baal Shem Tov's friend silent? Why was Bontsha silent? Why was Rabbi Nahman silent? Why was Noah silent? Why is God so often silent in the face of human tragedy? The answer is the same in every case. Were God to reverse His decree, were the natural order to be suspended at the importuning of a *tzaddik*, then the earth would revert to its original chaotic state, to *tohu va-vohu*. One of the dependable principles of God's Creation, the law of gravity, requires that if an innocent and lovely child falls out of a twentieth-story window, that child will die. If that law is suspended because of the piety and grief of its parents, if God catches that child and gently sets it down on the ground, then the law of gravity has been annulled. Then we can depend on nothing.

What would have been the result if God, the *tzaddik*, had cried out, if God had willed an end to the Shoah? The torture and killing might have ended, but at what cost? The cost would have been the ultimate Holocaust before which the actual Nazi Holocaust and all the other tragedies of humanity pale into insignificance. The price that humanity must pay for the intervention of God is the suspension of the natural order, of cause and effect, and consequently, of human free will.

What does it mean when God threatens to return the earth to primal chaos if the ministering angels and the *tzaddikim* are not silent? ("*Tzaddikim*," the Talmud teaches, "*are even greater than the ministering angels*" [*Sanhedrin* 93a].) It means a return to that primordial time when humanity had not yet been gifted with free will. It means human beings as puppets. For what is it that makes us human in the "image of God?" It is our ability to choose between good or evil, to choose between funding medical research and funding armaments, between bulging grain silos in Iowa and starvation in Africa, between equal opportunity for all and squalid urban ghettos. When we call upon God to intervene in human affairs, we surrender our divine potential as partners of God.

God and the *tzaddik* understand this and, understanding, they respond to human evil with silence. Andre Neher put it succinctly: "The cosmic silence is the sign not of an absence but, on the contrary, of a Presence" (*The Exile of the Word*, Philadelphia, 1981; p. 10). The "miraculous" cure of a mortally ill person is no proof for the existence of God, else why do others similarly afflicted die? Surely if God had stopped the Nazi trains from reaching the charnel houses, one would have every right to ask why God did not stop the Black Plague or environmental pollution. "*There is no utterance, and there are no words*" (Ps. 19:4), but the sun rises predictably each morning and the rivers fall predictably from the great continental divides and the crocuses appear in the spring. Thus do "*the heavens declare the glory of God, and the sky proclaims His handiwork*" (ibid., 2).

And so the *tzaddik* suffers and God suffers. And if a Shoah occurs, then God hangs with the innocent child, as in the vision of Elie Wiesel (*Night*, New York, 1969; p. 74ff.), dying slowly, agonizingly on the Nazi gallows.

The spiritual descendants of Abraham cry out and shake their fists and ask why, while those who have inherited the silence of Noah are mute, and their silence sustains God as He restrains Himself from annulling the horrendous results of human folly.

And so, which is the Jewish model, the justice-demanding Abraham or the quietistic Noah? Does God intend for us to "*sweep out evil from your midst*" (Deut. 13:6) or to remain passive in the face of evil, turning the other cheek (Matt. 5:39)? The overwhelming weight of Jewish tradition comes down on the side of Abraham. It is he, after all, who is designated in our liturgy as the first of the *avot* (patriarchs) and in Genesis as the first Hebrew (14:13) rather than the *tzaddik* Noah who preceded him by ten generations. But in a mystical response to the problem of human evil, Jewish folklore appropriated the model of Noah to provide a silent partner and friend for the withdrawn God. No matter how great the suffering that surrounds him, the *tzaddik* believes implicitly in the covenant made by God with Noah that "*never again shall all flesh be cut off*" (9:11). He believes, he accepts . . . and he is silent.

Turn 20

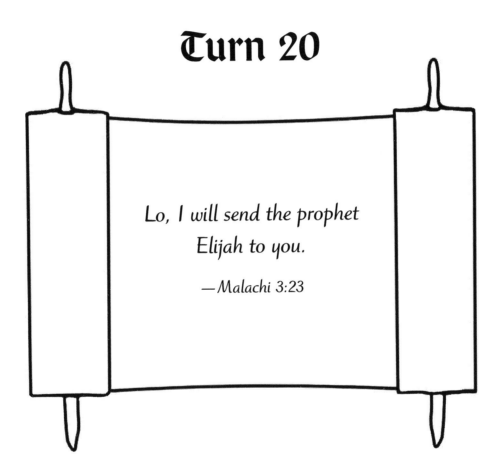

*Lo, I will send the prophet
Elijah to you.*

—Malachi 3:23

Yes, *that* Elijah, the one who comes to visit every Jewish home on Passover *Seder* night. But why? What does Elijah have to do with Passover? Why do we open the door for him, inspiring poignant memories in some and sniggers in others? What is there about Elijah that has made him one of the most ubiquitous figures in Jewish folklore? A good place to start this inquiry into the many traditions surrounding the figure of Elijah might be to repeat the opening lines of the "Elijah Cup" section in a popular modern Passover *Haggadah*:

> How many images this moment brings to mind,
> how many thoughts
> the memory of Elijah stirs in us. (*A Passover Haggadah*, CCAR)

What are those images and memories? And what is it that has made that plaintive *Eliyahu Ha-Navi* melody so poignantly familiar to generations of Jews?

The dramatic story of Elijah is told in six chapters at the end of 1 Kings and the beginning of 2 Kings. He is introduced in the first two verses of 1 Kings 17 as a Tishbite, a Gileadite, and a prophet (as reflected in the first three lines of the well-known song: *"Eliyahu ha-navi, Eliyahu ha-Tishbi, Eliyahu ha-Gileadi"*). The prophetic status of Elijah, like that of his successor, Elisha, and like Nathan and a few others of lesser importance who preceded them, was rather different from that of Isaiah, Jeremiah, Ezekiel, and those prophets whose messages have a prominent place in the biblical canon. These latter were literary prophets in that they wrote or dictated their prophecies which then became books of the Bible. Elijah was a miracle worker and a messenger of God, but he left no writings. We might call him and those others mentioned in connection with him nonliterary or preliterary prophets.

Elijah's first mission was to Ahab, king of Israel, *"who did what was displeasing to Adonai, more than all who preceded him"* (1 Kings 16:30). God instructed Elijah to tell Ahab that there would be a drought in the land of Israel which would last until Elijah prayed to God for rain. Elijah then, having to flee the wrath of Ahab, went into hiding in the desert across the Jordan where the first of his numerous miracles occured; he was fed by ravens.

That miracle was immediately followed by two others, both of which prefigure miracles by Elijah's disciple, Elisha, which in turn prefigure miracles ascribed to Jesus in the Christian Bible. He made a widow's handful of flour and drop of oil last through three years of drought, sustaining her family, and he revived the widow's dead son. (See essay, *Tell me all the wonderful things that Elisha has done.*) After three years, Elijah reappeared to King Ahab and set up a dramatic confrontation with the prophets of Baal on Mount Carmel. The pagan prophets prepared a bull for sacrifice and then appealed frenziedly but futilely to their gods to send down fire. That lack of response is described in the text in words that have become a popular Hebrew catch phrase indicating an absence of response: *"Ein kol v'ein oneh* (There was no sound and no reply)."

Elijah then doused his sacrificial bull with pitcher after pitcher of water and called on God to send down fire.

> *Then fire from Adonai descended and consumed the burnt offering, the wood, the stones and the earth; and it licked up the water that was in the trench. When they saw this, all the people flung themselves on their faces and cried out: "Adonai alone is God; Adonai alone is God."* (1 Kings 18:38-39)

The image of that contest on Mount Carmel etched itself so deeply into the mythos of Israel that it created a folk hero whose exploits have been celebrated in art, prose, song, and especially religious ritual. If you visit the Roman Catholic Carmelite monastery of Mukhraka (south of Haifa) today, you will find a statue of their patron saint, Elijah, and be told that this was the spot where Elijah defeated the prophets of Baal. If you attend the *Yom Kippur Ne'ilah* service in any synagogue in the world, you will hear the concluding cry of the cantor and congregation, echoing Elijah: "*Adonai hu ha-Elohim* (Adonai alone is God)." These Christian and Jewish homages to Elijah, though, are only the beginning. Before we go on to other fascinating customs that derive from the saga of Elijah, we'll take a look at the rest of the text.

When Ahab told his pagan wife, Jezebel, how Elijah had defeated, and subsequently slain, all the prophets of Baal, she vowed to kill him and so it was again necessary for him to flee. This time he fled to the Negev wilderness, depressed, hungry, and ready to die, but there again he was miraculously fed. And then his faith and spirits were revived when God sent a thunderous wind, a fire, and an earthquake, followed by a message in the well-known *"still, small voice."*

Elijah reacted to all of this by crying out: "I am moved by zeal for Adonai, the God of Hosts, for the Israelites have forsaken Your covenant." (Keep these words in mind, we shall see how they inspired another Jewish folk custom many centuries later.) God then responded to this outburst by giving Elijah a new mission: the anointing of a new king for neighboring Aram and a new king, Jehu, to replace Ahab. It was during the accomplishment of this dynastic mission that Elijah met the man who was to become his successor prophet and miracle worker, Elisha.

My favorite from among the several Elijah stories is the only one that deals with a matter of social justice, the well-known story of Naboth's vineyard (1 Kings 22). The confrontation between prophet and king in this story is reminiscent of the prophet Nathan's confrontation with King David after he had seduced Bathsheba, the wife of Uriah the Hittite (2 Sam. 11 and 12). In the Elijah story, it is King Ahab who commits a heinous sin, coveting a neighbor's vineyard and then, at the instigation of Jezebel, having him executed and taking possession of his vineyard. Elijah demanded justice, accusing Ahab: *"Would you murder and take possession?"* And then, as David did a century or so earlier, he confessed his sin and humbled himself before God. As for punishments, in the case of David, his illegitimate son was killed and the kingdom of his grandson, Rehoboam, was split; as for Ahab, his wife was killed and his son Ahaziah fell in battle after a two-year reign.

The book of 2 Kings begins with the final miracle story involving Elijah, and it is a rather ugly one, paralleled soon after in the Elisha stories. King Ahaziah sends a captain and a company of soldiers to bring Elijah to him so that he could ask the prophet whether his wounds would be fatal. When the captain ordered Elijah to come with him, Elijah called down a fire from heaven that consumed the captain and his troops. The same was repeated with a second captain and company. A third captain then approached rather more warily and with respect, and Elijah agreed to accompany him. Then, when he finally confronted Ahaziah, he told him that he would indeed die for his sins. (Just one chapter later, after Elisha inherited the prophetic mantle from Elijah, some children made fun of him because of his baldness. Elisha responded by cursing them. "*Thereupon, two she-bears came out of the woods and mangled forty-two of the children*" (2 Kings 2:24).

Forgive me if I use the Christian term, *assumption*, to describe the final episode of the Elijah saga. In Christianity, the assumption refers to the taking up of Jesus' mother, Mary, into heaven, body and soul. But whereas the Christian assumption story is not to be found in the Christian Bible but rather in a fifth-century apocryphal treatise (and fifteen centuries later declared a "revealed" dogma by Pope Pius X), the Elijah assumption story is not only told in the Bible but it is the essential element that transformed Elijah from a miracle-working zealot into a source of comfort and hope from the fifth pre-Christian century to our own day.

What happened in the fifth pre-Christian century? That was when the prophet Malachi lived, and Malachi* concluded his brief book (the final prophetic book in the traditional Hebrew canon) with a prophecy about "the end of days" when

> *Lo, I will send the prophet Elijah to you before the coming of the awesome, fearful day of Adonai. He shall reconcile parents with children and children with parents, so that when I come, I do not strike the whole land with utter destruction.*

Where did Malachi get the idea that Elijah would be the precursor of the "*fearful day of Adonai?*" From the fact that Elijah was the only biblical hero who never died! The Bible is quite specific about the deaths of Adam, Noah, the patriarchs, Joseph, Moses, Aaron, and David. Nowhere is there even a hint that a human, no matter how righteous, was anything other than mortal. But in the case of Elijah,

---

*   Scholarly opinion is divided about the name Malachi. Some believe that it was the actual name of the last of the prophets, while others believe that it is a descriptive appellation meaning "My messenger."

*a fiery chariot with fiery horses suddenly appeared, and Elijah . . . went
up to heaven in a whirlwind.*

And so Malachi selected the one and only prophetic character who was not
only able to call down an awesome series of miracles from God, seemingly at
will, but the only character who was "assumed" into heaven, body and soul.
There had to be a reason why God decided to immortalize Elijah. What might
that reason have been? Because as an immortal, Elijah would be available to
return to earth "*at the end of days*" with a message of reconciliation that would
inspire the people to return to God, thus avoiding the "*utter destruction*" that
God had promised Noah would never again occur.

It was not only God, though, who preserved Elijah for his great task "*at the
end of days.*" Jewish folklore needed a character who might intercede for
the powerless and bring comfort through all the centuries of persecution
and wandering. And that need produced a massive folklore, midrashic and
postmidrashic, that not only described the ongoing appearances of an often-
incognito Elijah when needed but also involved him in some of the most
basic and beloved of Jewish rituals. It is worthy of note that while the books
of Kings ascribe far more miracles to Elisha than to Elijah, the midrashic
literature is far more interested in Elijah. And as far as postmidrashic
literature is concerned, while Elisha hardly ever appears, Elijah is ubiquitous.

There are four venerable Jewish traditions that involve the presence of Elijah
and that are practiced by, or are at least familiar to, virtually all Jews to this
very day. And they are the following:

Havdalah (the service marking the conclusion of Shabbat)—According to A.
Z. Idelsohn, the noted authority on Jewish liturgy, by the eleventh century
"there were songs of Elijah sung by all Jewish communities on the outgoing
of Sabbath." Today it is customary to sing the popular song, *Eliyahu Ha-Navi*,
during the *Havdalah* service in most Jewish communities, but in Sephardic
communities, there is a rather elaborate Elijah ritual that is the very heart of that
service. This ritual begins with the singing of *Eliyahu Ha-Navi* but then goes on
to the recitation of a twenty-eight line *piyyut* (liturgical poem) glorifying Elijah,
yearning for his redemptive return and concluding with the "*end of days*" verses.

Why did Elijah become such an important part of *Havdalah*? Most likely
because Shabbat is supposed to be a foretaste of the messianic age. There

are several customs that are intended to prolong the spirit of Shabbat, even after the Saturday night skies turn dark. Living in often hostile environments through most of history since the Diaspora, Jews valued Shabbat not only as a sacred day reminiscent of Creation but also as a respite from the trials and tribulations of the onerous workweek. They deeply regretted the departure of Shabbat and consoled themselves with references to a better time when Elijah would come, bind up all wounds, and declare the advent of the Messiah.

Birkat Ha-Mazon (prayers of thanks after meals)—In the same spirit as the above, a verse was added to the *Birkat Ha-Mazon*, probably also around the eleventh century, petitioning God to send Elijah with the news of the forthcoming redemption: "*Harahaman hu yishlach lanu et Eliyahi Ha-Navi* (May the Merciful One send us Elijah the Prophet, whose memory brings us blessing, so that he may tell us the good news of redemption, victories and comfort)."

Berit Milah (covenantal circumcision service)—At the beginning of the *Berit Milah* service, after the child is brought in, the *Mohel* (circumciser) places him on a special chair, often elaborately decorated, and announces, "This is the chair of Elijah." Why a special chair for Elijah? The custom derives from an eighth-century midrashic work, *Pirkei de-Rabbi Eliezer* (chap. 29), which comments on the story in 1 Kings 19 in which Elijah complains to God that "*the Israelites have forsaken Your covenant.*" Because of this accusation, uttered by Elijah in anger, God commanded Elijah to be present at every circumcision ceremony so that he would be a witness to this dramatic evidence of the loyalty of the Jewish people to the *Berit* (covenant).

It is unfortunate that while the custom of the Elijah chair is still observed at almost every *Berit*, the *Mohel* does not usually take the time to explain about the connection of Elijah to the ceremony but simply makes the perfunctory announcement, "This is the chair of Elijah." A folk belief that derives from Elijah's presence at the *Berit* is that Elijah checks each eight-day-old child to see if he might be the Messiah. In this custom, as in those above, one sees evidence of the eternal yearning of the Jewish people for the Messiah or, as with most modern Jews, the yearning for a messianic age of liberation, righteousness, and justice.

Passover Seder—This is the best known and most beloved of all the instances where the memory of Elijah is invoked but it is also, I believe, the most misunderstood. While it is true, as most believe, that Elijah is welcomed to the

Seder as the herald of the messianic age, it is not true that this is his primary function. Why, then, is he an essential presence at every *Seder*? Because there was a disagreement among the sages who established the rituals of the *Seder* as to whether there should be four cups of wine or five. So?

The custom of the multiple cups derives from the promises made by God to the enslaved Israelites in Exodus, chapter 6. The text reads, "*I will free you . . .*", *I will deliver you . . .*", "*I will redeem you . . .*", "*and I will take you to be My people.*" These four promises follow one after the other in rapid succession in verses six and seven. Then after an intervening verse, we read, "*I will bring you into the land.*" Each cup of wine is a symbol of the joy that we feel as the beneficiaries of God's promises. But is that fifth promise actually connected to the prior four or is it a separate promise? On this the rabbis could not agree. Some said that there should be four cups in honor of four promises and some said five cups for five promises.

There is an Aramaic word *teku* that is used in the Talmud to indicate that the rabbis could not reach a decision on a matter under discussion. The decision as to the number of cups was left *teku*, but provisionally the Passover *Haggadah* prescribes four cups (possibly as a parallel to the four questions and the four sons). But just in case there really should be five cups, the *Haggadah* prescribes that we should have a symbolic fifth cup of wine. How did this symbolic fifth cup come to be known as "the cup of Elijah?" Ah, that takes us back to that word *teku*.

Nobody is certain of the derivation of the word *teku*. The noted Israeli lexicographer, Abraham Even-Shoshan, suggests that it might derive from *tekum* (it will stand, i.e., it will remain a question). But then he goes on to explain that there is a folk etymology that has it that *teku* is an acronym for "*Tishbi yetaretz kushiot v-abayot* (the Tishbite, i.e., Elijah, will answer all unresolved questions)." And so, according to this folk belief, the first thing that Elijah will do, when he returns to the midst of the Jewish people to proclaim the advent of the messianic age, is to explain all those questions of Jewish law that the rabbis were not able to explain. I personally doubt that this was the original meaning of *teku*, but I love this folk etymology and I trot it out each year at my own *Seder*.

I have made mention of the ubiquitousness of Elijah in the midrash and later Jewish folk literature. A small sampling:

- Rabbi Beroka Hozaa was once in the market place of Bei-Lephet and he happened to meet Elijah, the prophet. [Taking advantage of this fortuitous meeting,] he asked him, "Is there anyone in this market who is worthy of eternal reward?" Answered Elijah: "Those two men are worthy of eternal reward . . ." (Rabbi Beroka then ascertains that they bring joy into people's lives.) (Talmud, *Taanit* 25a)

- It happened that a pious man who had a virtuous wife became impoverished. and had to hire himself out as a day laborer. Once when he was plowing in a field, he met Elijah, the prophet, dressed as an Arab . . . (As the story proceeds, the incognito Elijah offers him six prosperous years which, because of the charitable acts of his wife, are extended indefinitely.) (*Yalkut Shimoni, Ruth* 4)

- (A man who was guilty of some offense against the government took refuge in the home of Rabbi Joshua ben Levi in Lod. When officers followed him there, they threatened to destroy the entire city if the guilty man were not handed over to them. Rabbi Joshua felt that he had no choice, and so he delivered the man to the officers.) Until that time, Elijah used to appear regularly to Rabbi Joshua, but after this incident, Elijah no longer appeared. Rabbi Joshua fasted for thirty days, and then Elijah reappeared to him. Rabbi Joshua asked him, "Why did you stop appearing to me?" And Elijah answered, "It is not my custom to be friendly with informers." (The midrash goes on to explain that while others might follow the letter of the law, exemplars like Rabbi Joshua must live up to a higher ethic.) (*Genesis Rabbah* 94)

- Rabbi Joshua ben Levi said, "Once I was walking on the road, and I met Elijah, the prophet, who asked me if I would like to stand at the entrance to Gehenna [to see what was going on inside]. I said, "Yes" . . . (The story goes on to describe the punishments meted out to varieties of sinners, all involving torture to different parts of their bodies.) (Late midrashic collection, Tractate *Gehinom*)

- (Rabbi Kahana who was very poor and reduced to selling baskets to women, was approached by a powerful woman who made lewd advances to him. On the pretext of preparing himself, he climbed up to the roof and hurled himself to the ground.) Elijah came, caught him and then reproached him: "You have troubled me to come a very long distance [to save you]." He answered, "I was forced to do it due to my poverty." And so Elijah gave him a basketful of dinars. (Talmud, *Kiddushin* 40a)

And finally, Elijah suddenly appears in the epilogue to one of the best-known passages in the Talmud, the incident known as the oven of Aknai (Talmud, *Bava Metzia* 59b). In this story, the most prominent rabbis of the early second century were arguing a point of law when a heavenly voice interrupted their discussion by announcing that Rabbi Eliezer's position was the correct one. Rabbi Joshua replied by urging the sages to disregard the heavenly voice since the Torah was no longer in heaven. The point of the story is that correct law can only be determined rationally, i.e., by discussion and the majority vote of the rabbis, not by miracles. This is the classic rabbinic defense of the right of Torah interpretation by later generations of scholars. The story concludes with this vignette:

- Rabbi Nathan met Elijah and asked him: "What did the Holy One, blessed be He, do in that hour [i.e., when the rabbis rejected divine intervention into their deliberations]? Elijah replied, "He laughed [with joy] and said: 'My children have defeated Me! My children have defeated Me!'"

Later folk literature often introduced Elijah as the savior in the all-too-frequent situations down through the centuries when communities of Jews were in dire straits. Elijah would appear out of nowhere, often incognito, and foil the wicked plot. Again, why Elijah? Because he was the hero who could call down miracles, he was the intimate of God who never died, he was the intercessor who would plead the cause of his people with zeal. And so Jewish tradition venerated Elijah and invited him into the family circle at the end of every Sabbath, at every meal, at circumcisions and most notably, at the most dramatic of all home rituals, the Passover *Seder*. On all of these occasions Jews yearn for the day when "*Lo, I will send the prophet Elijah to you.*

Turn 21

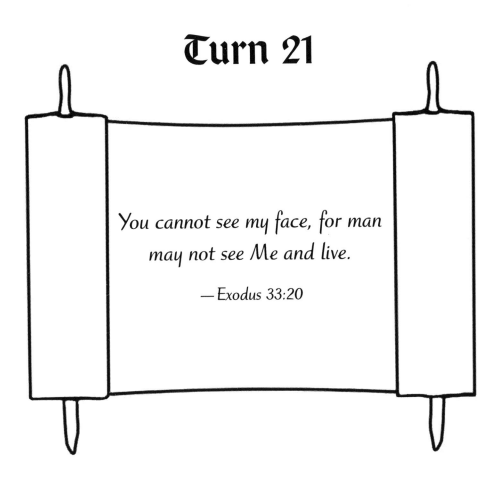

You cannot see my face, for man may not see Me and live.

— Exodus 33:20

One of the basic tenets of Jewish theology is that God has no body, no physical attributes whatsoever. The well-known fourteenth-century hymn *Yigdal Elohim Hai*, which is a poetic restatement of the Maimonidean creed, puts it quite nicely: "*Ein lo demut ha-guf v'eino guf . . .*—[God] has no physical shape nor a body." That this was not an easy concept for the early Israelites to accept is attested to by the many incidents of backsliding, of reverting to idol worship that we find scattered throughout the Bible—the golden calf, the worship of the Moabite Baal Peor, by Rachel and Michal with their *teraphim*, numerous incidents of reversion to idolatry in the era of the Judges, to say nothing of the many prophets who over and over again had to rebuke the people for their worship of graven images. Typical is this passage from the prophecy of Hosea, following his description of the love that God had lavished on Israel:

> *Thus will I punish her for the days of the Baalim,*
> *On which she brought them offerings; . . . forgetting Me.* (2:15)

Maimonides explains away the entire sacrificial cult to which so many chapters of the Torah are devoted by saying that animal sacrifice to a seemingly hungry God was a necessary step on the road from idolatry to the pure worship of God for the early Israelites. It must have been very difficult for people who were not schooled in the subtleties of abstract thought to conceive an all-powerful God who refused to be seen or even represented. And so, according to this line of Maimonidean logic, God commanded Moses to give the people a system of animal sacrifice very similar to the sacrificial cults connected to the worship of Baal and Dagon and Moloch and all the other gods of the surrounding nations, with a mystically garbed priesthood and a sanctuary, all of the trappings of idolatry, *without* the idols. Even Moses himself on at least one occasion became confused by the fine line between idolatry and the pure worship of an incorporeal God when, in order to bring an end to a plague of serpents, he *"made a copper serpent and mounted it on a standard"* (Num. 21:9) for the people to contemplate.

One can only sympathize with Moses who, while trying to wean the people and himself from idolatry, could employ only the vocabulary that was available to him, a vocabulary that lacked words like incorporeality or metaphysics. And it was not only in ancient times that Israelites had difficulty with the concept of an unseen God. One of the great liturgical poems by the twelfth-century poet-philosopher, Judah Ha-Levi, opens with the cry:

> *Yah ana emtzaacha*—O God, where can I find you?
> *Mekomcha naalah veneelam*—Your abode is lofty and hidden.

This plaint was repeated in the liturgy of modern Reform Judaism in a meditation by Rabbi Louis Witt that asks,

> O God, how can we know You? Where can we find You? You are as close to us as breathing, yet You are farther than the farthermost star. You are as mysterious as the vast solitudes of night, yet as familiar to us as the light of the sun. To Moses you said: "You cannot see my face, but I will make all my goodness pass before you." (Originally published in the Union Prayer Book [1961] and revised for the new Reform Prayer Book, *Mishkan T'filah*.)

We shall presently return to this response by God to Moses's search for the divine essence, but it is important to recognize at the very outset of our own search that every generation of Jews, from Moses to our own day, has been involved in that often frustrating and even agonizing search. That intelligent people, even in the twenty-first century, often feel a deep need to envision the object of their adoration is attested to by the icons that are ubiquitous in Roman Catholicism and Eastern Orthodoxy, to say nothing of the images, great and small, of the non-Christian Eastern religions. And even in the iconoclastic Jewish community, there are many who find it necessary to carry amulets inscribed with the words, if not the image, of God in order to feel secure.

One of the reasons why theological speculation was not a basic part of Judaism until possibly the tenth century is that Jewish sages found it difficult to convey in words the concept of God's reality to people who yearned for something concrete, for at least a glimpse of divinity. Theology is not a Jewish science.

Rabbis tend to talk and write about ritual practices, social issues, and ethics but rarely about the nature of God. I was told recently by the chairman of a rabbinic search committee that in their interviews with about a dozen candidates for their pulpit, only one of them mentioned God. This is by no means to suggest that those other candidates, and rabbis generally, don't believe in God. I, for one, believe deeply in God. I love God, but I confess that I rarely speak about God. Why? Because I lack the words that would enable me, in a twenty-minute sermon, to convey my God belief without reducing God to something like Michelangelo's bearded, Zeus-like caricature.

Those few medieval rabbinic sages whom we think of as theologians—Saadiah, Judah Ha-Levi, Maimonides, and a few others—were, in fact, not theologians by choice. They were rather apologists; they wrote about the nature of God reluctantly, in response to what they considered to be the erroneous and challenging theologies of Islam and Christianity. Jewish sages have always preferred to talk about mitzvot, about what a Jew should *do* rather than what she or he should *believe*. If you want to reduce that assertion to a slogan, it would be that Jews are concerned with *deed*, not *creed*.

Of course, this reticence about the personalization of God creates a problem for those who, like myself, find prayer to be efficacious. Prayer all too often uses human terminology in the attempt to draw the worshiper closer to God. Can one, in fact, offer even the least anthropomorphic prayer without the suggestion that while the worshiper is praying, God is listening? As soon as we utter one word of prayer, we are involved in a paradox; we, rationalists, become mystics. If we address God, then God becomes a partner in dialogue, from our lips, as it were, to God's ears.

The prevailing Jewish hesitation to speculate about the nature of the divine or even to speak about God was noted by the nineteenth-century French historian and biblical scholar, Ernest Renan, who wrote of the Jews:

> What a strange people. They gave God to the world and barely believe in Him. They founded the hope of man in a kingdom of heaven, yet all their wise men tell us that we must occupy ourselves only with earthly things.

An observer of American Jewry today might come to the same conclusion about this strange unwillingness to verbalize a belief in God as did Renan. And in fact, many Jews, then as now, desert the ranks of religious Jewry precisely because they have difficulty with God-language. Unable to accept traditional references to the nature of God as poetic metaphor, they disparage faith as superstition. And on the other hand, of course, we have Jews whose belief in God is so totally anthropomorphic that they repel other Jews who are in earnest search for some rational formulation of the nature of God.

Paradox is a part of the pleasure, and the exquisite agony, of Jewish existence and it is, of course, nothing new. The entire magnificent book of Job is an attempt to solve the mystery of God. Is God involved in the affairs of human beings? Is there reward and punishment? Can a mere mortal hope to understand the workings of God's "mind?" Listen to God's "response" to Job's audacity in thinking that he might comprehend the nature of God:

> *Who is this who darkens counsel, speaking without knowledge?*
> *Gird your loins like a man; I will ask and you will inform Me.*
> *Where were you when I laid the foundations of the earth?*
> *Speak if you have understanding.* (38:2-4)

And Job's pitiful but utterly human response:

> *Indeed, I spoke without understanding,*
> *Of things beyond me which I did not know . . .*
> *Therefore, I recant and relent,*
> *Being but dust and ashes.* (42:3-6)

In the second century, Rabbi Akiba, in his search for an understanding of the nature of God, came up with as paradoxical a formulation as has ever become a basic tenet of a religion: "*All is foreseen [by God], yet free will is given [to humanity].*" How can we human beings have the gift of free will if God knows in advance what choices we will make? Paradox. And then there was Maimonides, widely accepted as the greatest of Jewish theologians, who in effect, threw up his hands and said, "God has no attributes." Those Jews who go to their synagogues and piously utter their prayers in a rote fashion without ever pausing to wrestle with the paradoxical nature of God have ceded any claim to involvement in the eternal Jewish search.

Nowhere in the Bible is that search so marvelously articulated as in the doubly paradoxical confrontation between God and Moses at Sinai when the Israelites set up an idol, a golden calf, while Moses was receiving the commandments. In chapter 32 of Exodus, God angrily informs Moses that He intends to destroy Israel for its lack of faith in the very aftermath of the miraculous Exodus from Egyptian bondage. Moses is forced to employ all of his rhetorical skill to change God's mind and this, of course, is paradox number one. "*Adonai renounced the punishment He had planned to bring upon His people.*" How is it possible that an all-knowing God could be surprised by the actions of His people? And how is it possible that having made up His "mind," God then changes His mind? (We are reminded of the verse in Numbers 23:19: "*God is not like . . . a mortal who might change his mind.*")

It is upon the second paradox, the one that is the main substance of Exodus 33, that I want to focus. After Moses, in effect, succeeds in changing God's mind about the destruction of Israel, he feels that for his own sense of security, he needs to know more about God. And so he asks,

> *If I have truly gained Your favor, pray let me know Your ways, that I may know You and continue in Your favor . . . And Adonai said to Moses: I will also do this thing that you have asked; for you have truly gained my favor.*

Now we must remember that in the verse immediately preceding the above, we were told that Moses met God regularly in a tent and that "*Adonai would speak to Moses face to face, as one man speaks to another.*" And so what was it that Moses, having already seen the face of God [!!!], really wanted when, pressing God further, he asked, "*Let me behold Your presence!*" Hadn't Moses already seen God's presence? What more did he want? It is in God's answer to these questions that we may begin to understand what it means to "see" God. God answered,

> *I will make all My goodness pass before you as I proclaim My name before you. I will be gracious to whom I will be gracious and show compassion to whom I will show compassion. But, He said, you cannot see My face, for man may not see Me and live.*

And that paradoxical statement is followed by what has to be (with the possible exception of Ezekiel 1:26-28) the most anthropomorphic passage in the entire Bible. God continues,

See, there is a place near Me. Station yourself on the rock and, as My presence passes by, I will put you in the cleft of the rock and shield you with My hand until I have passed by. Then I will take My hand away and you will see My back, but My face must not be seen.

Imagine! Whoever wrote those verses—Moses or Joshua or some priest or scribe who lived three thousand or so years ago—believed that Moses and God met regularly in a tent and conferred there. How did they confer? "*Face to face, as one man speaks to another.*" And so God, it would seem, has a face, a visage, that was seen by a mortal. Moses was, of course, no ordinary mortal, but he was a man who "*may not see Me and live.*"

But did Moses, in fact, see a physical aspect of God? If so, the paradox: Why did he then ask to see God's presence? Are we dealing here with bad editing? Or are we possibly dealing with two different documents, one of which promotes Moses to the ranks of the divine by having him confer with God as one person speaks to another and the other of which informs Moses that like all mortals, he cannot see God? Even if we are dealing with two separate documents that were, at some later time, stitched together, there is one major area of agreement. And that is that, whether a human may see the face of God or not, God has a face! Clearly, if God says, "*You cannot see my face*" and then goes on to refer to His "hand" which will shield Moses and His "back" which Moses is allowed to see, then God has a form! After this divine anatomy lesson, it would seem that God does, in fact, have a physical presence.

But there is another way to understand this paradoxical text, a way that is as spiritual and metaphysical as anything written in all the years since the recension of the Torah. Let's take another look at the text. Moses asks to see God's presence and God answers, "*I will make all My goodness pass before you . . . I will be gracious to whom I will be gracious and show compassion to whom I will show compassion. But you cannot see My face.*" What does this mean?

At a time when Israel was surrounded by idolatry, fetishism, animism, and the grossest barbarity, a religious genius suggested that the way to "see" God was through the acts of God, the goodness of God. Human beings may not see My face, but "*I will make all My goodness pass before you.*"

How can we know God? Where can we find God? Through acts of goodness, through graciousness and compassion. And what should this mean to the person who is seeking a glimpse of God, to a person who is striving, as we are taught in Leviticus 19, to "be holy as God is holy?" It means that as God is merciful, *we* must be merciful; as God is gracious, *we* must be gracious; as God heals the sick, *we* must heal the sick; as God lifts up the fallen, so must *we* lift up the fallen; as God feeds the hungry, *we* must feed the hungry. This is how we "see" God.

And so why the references in that amazing passage to God's face and hand and back? Because the language of abstraction and metaphysics had not yet evolved. What is remarkable about that passage in Exodus is *not* the divine anatomy catalogue but rather the beginning of a theology that is the very opposite of idolatry, a theology that inspires *imitatio dei*—the attempt to act in the image of God.

Does this answer the problem of evil in the world? No, we are still—like Job, like Elie Wiesel, like Harold Kushner who asked why bad things happen to good people—grappling with this mystery, and it is possible that we may never find the answer. But it is eminently clear that the more people who are inspired to imitate the revealed presence of God, God's goodness, graciousness, and compassion, the better our world will be. We cannot see God's face, we cannot understand all the paradoxes of the universe, but we can see God's goodness revealed to us in thousands of ways every day of our lives.

Returning to that wonderfully perceptive meditation by Rabbi Witt,

> When justice burns within us like a flaming fire, when love evokes willing sacrifice from us, when, to the last full measure of selfless devotion, we demonstrate our belief in the ultimate triumph of truth and righteousness, then Your goodness enters our lives and we can begin to change the world; and then You live within our hearts, and we through righteousness behold Your presence.

Turn 22

Ephraim is My darling son,
a child of delight.

—Jeremiah 31:19 (20)

One of the longstanding calumnies against the Hebrew Bible is that it posits a vengeful and bloodthirsty God. The standard proofs: the plagues rained down upon the Egyptians and their subsequent drowning in the Sea of Reeds, the eternal vengeance decreed against Amalek, the threat of punishment to the third and fourth generations of sinners, the dynastic wars in the books of Samuel and Kings, and finally, the destruction of Jerusalem and the exile, punishments meted out by that vindictive "Old Testament" God. And of course, this is contrasted with the God of love of the "New Testament."

I have heard Christian polemicists citing, as proof for the assertion that the "New Testament" God is a God of love, the story of Jesus's response to the hostile Pharisee (Matt. 22:34ff) who asked him what was the greatest commandment in the law. Jesus's answer: "*You shall love the Lord your God . . . and a second is like it. You shall love your neighbor as yourself.*" These are indeed beautiful lessons about the love of God and the love of neighbor, but what the denigrator of the Hebrew Bible omits to mention is that Jesus was, of course, quoting from the Torah (Deut. 6:5 and Lev. 19:18) as any Jewish teacher of that time might have done.

There are no stories of warfare in the Christian testament because the Gospels are products of the time when the Roman Empire was all-powerful. To make war or to rebel against Rome, as the Judeans discovered in the year 70 and again with the Bar Kokhba uprising two generations later, was futile. And Paul did not hesitate, in his *Epistle to the Romans* (12:19), to invoke the vengeance of God while asserting that humans, in order to avoid it, should practice love. And how did he describe the way that people should act in their relations with their neighbors? Again, by quoting from the Hebrew Bible (Prov. 25:21f). One would hope that the calumny about the Hebrew Bible's God of vengeance versus the New Testament's God of love, an aspect of Christian supersecessionism, would have been laid to rest after Vatican II; but somehow it refuses to die.

If there is any one theme that runs through the entire Hebrew Bible, it is the tension between the God of loving mercy and the God of absolute justice. Early on, the rabbis noted the use of the name *Elohim* for God in chapter 1 of Genesis and the use of *Adonai* or *Adonai Elohim* in the second chapter. Modern scholarship explains the use of different names for God as proof that the stories in the Torah, particularly the two accounts of Creation in chapters 1 and 2 of Genesis, come from different sources and that they were later interwoven by some priestly editor into the Torah that Jews have read since about the fourth pre-Christian century. But for the early rabbis, the presence of the two names indicated the two preeminent characteristics of God: loving mercy and justice. The Midrash teaches that if God had created the world only with loving mercy (i.e., as *Adonai*), sin would prevail in our world but that if God had created the world only with justice (i.e., as *Elohim*), humanity could not survive. And so God combined these two essential characteristics in order to create a world that could survive.

One may accept or reject this clever midrashic explanation, but the fact remains that we find the conflict between God's loving mercy and God's absolute justice on virtually every page of Hebrew scripture. Rather than a long list of quotations, I would cite as typical the contrast in the second commandment (Exod. 20:5f) between the punishment for those who worship other gods and the reward for those who are faithful to the God of Israel. Not only will the idolaters themselves be punished but their children as well to the third and fourth generations. But *"I will show loving mercy to the thousandth generation of those who love me and keep My commandments."* And in the prophetic literature, in the books of Isaiah, Hosea, and Jeremiah in particular, we find the most dire threats against Israel for their misconduct, but punishment by the God of justice is always followed by reconciliation with the God of loving mercy. Sin, punishment, and then reconciliation—a prefiguring of Hegelian dialectic: thesis, antithesis, and synthesis.

Having noted this biblical tension between God's loving mercy and God's justice, I would be less than candid if I did not concede that it is God's attribute of justice that is most evident in the earliest centuries of Israel's saga. But the prophets, for the most part, supplied the necessary corrective. A prime example of this prophetic corrective may be found in the reactions of both

Ezekiel and Jeremiah to the idea, plainly stated in the second commandment, that children will be made to suffer for the sins of their parents.

The two prophets quote what seems to have been a popular proverb in their days, "*Parents eat sour grapes, and their children's teeth are set on edge,*" and they both proceed to demolish it. Jeremiah (31:29f) states quite simply that this old proverb will no longer apply in the ideal future when people will be punished only for their own sins, not for those of their parents. And this assurance may also be found in the book of Deuteronomy (24:16), probably written during the lifetime of Jeremiah.

Ezekiel, though, devotes an entire chapter (18) to the refutation, itemized with example after example, of that old proverb. He describes the acts of righteous parents with wicked children and wicked parents with righteous children and comes to the unequivocal conclusions that (1) each person shall be punished or rewarded for his own acts and (2) that repentance is always available to the wicked; if the former sinner "*does what is just and right, such a person shall save his life.*" One would hope that the calumny about the vengeful God of the Jews would have been laid to rest by these prophets who had the courage and moral authority to, in effect, abrogate a clause from the Ten Commandments in order to eradicate the idea of a vindictive God.

Nowhere is the doctrine of a forgiving God more clearly spelled out than in that same chapter from Ezekiel where the prophet says in the name of God: "*Is it My desire that a wicked person shall die? It is rather that he shall turn back from his ways and live.*" This prophetic statement is so important a part of Judaism to this very day that it is repeated several times in the atonement liturgy of Yom Kippur. No, the belief in a loving and forgiving God did not originate with Christianity. If Jesus preached that message, it was because he learned it from the Jewish scriptures which he heard as a child in the synagogues of Galilee.

Since early childhood, I have thought of God as a loving but demanding parent. No doubt this image was colored by my particular family situation, but also influential in my personal ideation of God was a biblical verse that became "mine" at the age of seven when I joined my cantor father's High Holy Day choir as the boy soprano. The choirs in Orthodox synagogues must be all male and so, since the very idea of castrati is repugnant to Judaism, alto and soprano lines are sung by prepubescent boys. There are many stories in the literature of east European Jewry about itinerant cantors who would travel from synagogue to synagogue accompanied by a bass and a "zinger'l," a little boy singer. I was the "zinger'l" in my father's male choir from the age of seven until my Bar Mitzvah. And my favorite solo, the one that was guaranteed to elicit sobs from the women's gallery, was "*Ha-vein yakir li Ephraim* (Ephraim is my darling son, a child of delight)."

Who was the Ephraim that the prophet Jeremiah referred to with such tender love? Ephraim was the name of the preeminent tribe of the northern Israelite kingdom after the war that split the country during the reign of King Rehoboam. The terms *Israel* and *Ephraim* are used interchangeably to refer to the ten northern tribes, but *Ephraim* is the more familiar and poetic name. The original Ephraim for whom the tribe was named was, of course, the younger son of Joseph. The reader will recall, from the magnificent painting by Rembrandt if not from the Genesis text, that when the aged Jacob blessed the two sons of Joseph, he placed his right hand on the head of Ephraim, explaining to Joseph that the younger son would be the greater of the two. The prophets often chose to refer to the kingdom of Israel as Ephraim in much the same way as Frenchmen might refer to France as Marianne or Englishmen refer to England as Albion.

Long before I knew any of this and long before I had ever heard of the prophet Jeremiah, I was not only familiar with his poignant accolade to Ephraim, but I could also sing it in the original Hebrew and would do so enthusiastically at the slightest urging. To this very day, I experience moments of wistful nostalgia, accompanied by the "*Ha-vein yakir li*" melody, as I recall long-departed members of my childhood *shul*, all those honorary uncles and aunties and especially incidents—some joyful, some painful—with my father. I became emotionally attached to that verse from Jeremiah not only because it spoke of God's parental love, at a time when I was hungry for such love, but also because one of my two middle names was, in fact, Ephraim. Ironically, as much as I loved that solo and felt that it was "mine," I hated my extraneous name Ephraim and never used it. It did not help that I had an elderly cousin who, whenever he saw me, would cry out at the top of his voice, "Here comes little e-fry'em two eggs!"

There are, of course, many instances in the Bible where the relationship between God and the people of Israel is compared to the loving relationship between a husband and a wife rather than between a father and a son. The first two chapters of Hosea describe the love that God felt for Israel when they met in the wilderness of Sinai and then, after Israel's betrayal, the love that moved God to forgive and to reunite with Israel in an eternal covenant of marriage. Jeremiah too referred to that early virginal love (2:2) and then to the "*eternal love*" that developed between God, "the Lover" and Israel, "the Beloved" (31:3). The prophets and the psalmists employed both of these metaphors, lover-beloved and father-son extensively but the point was the same, that God's love for Israel will overcome even the worst offenses, that "*Adonai is compassionate and gracious, slow to anger, abounding in steadfast love*" (Ps. 103:8).

It is, though, the theology of the father-son relationship that has always spoken most meaningfully and poignantly to me. During the atonement ritual of Yom Kippur, I read the psalmist's words: "*As a father has compassion for his children, . . .*" and my heart melts. I yearn for God to heal all the wounds of the past and to teach me what it means to be a father "in the image of God." The prophet Malachi thought of God as father (see 1:6 and 2:10); Isaiah cried out to God, "*You are our father*," time after time (see 63:16 and 64:7). One of the most common names employed to address God is *Avinu* (our Father), both in the Bible and in the liturgy of Judaism. This intimate form of address was, of course, adopted by Christianity in the well-known *Pater Noster* prayer and elsewhere. And lest the reader think that the often misogynistic biblical authors were unsympathetic to mother-love also as a paradigm for God's love, there are beautiful passages in Isaiah (66:13 and 49:15 in particular) that focus on the mother-child relationship.

The father-son relationship that recurs to me most often, though, especially in private meditative moments is "*Ephraim is My darling son, a child of delight.*" I recall the many times during my childhood when I stormed out of our house after a tongue-lashing or a particularly rigorous punishment and ran down to the nearby beach. I would walk along the shore drive, where my tears would be replaced by the salty ocean mist on my cheeks, and I would plead my case with the Father of that "*child of delight.*" "I am Ephraim; I am the darling son. God loved Ephraim, even after all the sins. Why can't they love me?" And the poignant melody of my favorite solo would accompany my plaint as I walked down to the end of the beach and back. And after my solo? Then my father would take up the melody and continue with the text, "*My heart yearns for him; I will surely have compassion on him.*" And so, reassured, I would go home. And, indeed, it was true.

I often whispered and crooned my Ephraim solo when I held my own baby son, *and* my daughters, in my arms, along with the prayer that they be spared the anger that so often erodes the parent-child relationship. And to this day, when I am saddened by some turn of events, when I despair of the foibles of friends and family members and, yes, of governments, when I can imagine only suffering as the result, I am reassured that the God of parental love, who has been my lifelong companion and whose love I find in every chapter of scripture, will recall the delights of parenthood and grant us peace.

Turn 23

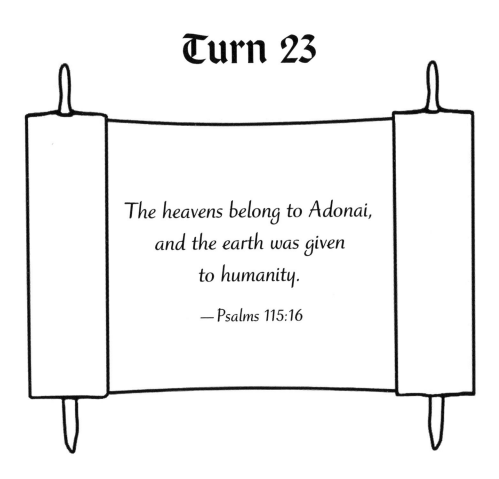

The heavens belong to Adonai,
and the earth was given
to humanity.

—Psalms 115:16

One of the high points of synagogue worship is the chanting of a series of psalms that are known collectively as *Hallel*, praise, as in *Halleluyah*. The great nineteenth-century German scholar, Rabbi Samson Raphael Hirsch, referred to *Hallel* as "the Jewish song of jubilation that has accompanied our wanderings of thousands of years, . . . strengthening us in times of sorrow and suffering, and filling our mouths with song of rejoicing in days of deliverance and triumph." The *Hallel* consists of Psalms 113 through 118, and it is a feature of almost all the festival morning services.

As if to emphasize the exultant spirit of *Hallel*, it is omitted as inappropriate from the solemn liturgy of the High Holy Days, and it is also omitted from the liturgy of the final days of Passover. This latter omission was decreed by the early rabbis because of a fanciful but sensitive Talmudic story (*Sanhedrin* 39b) that relates how God rebuked the ministering angels when they attempted to join in the singing of the jubilant song that Moses and Israel sang (Exod. 15) after the pursuing Egyptians were drowned. God stopped them, crying out, "My creatures are drowning in the sea, and you want to sing?" And so, after the joyful celebration of the Exodus on the first day of Passover, during which the entire *Hallel* is recited, two paragraphs are omitted for the rest of the festival. It is in this same spirit, in keeping with the injunction not to rejoice over the death of enemies (Prov. 24:17), that we pour off ten drops of wine from our cups of joy during the recitation of the ten plagues at the Passover *Seder*.

Since the second century *Hallel* has also been included in the liturgy of the new moon, and for a variety of questionable reasons, it is omitted from the celebration of Purim. In general, though, we can say that the jubilant recitation of *Hallel* is one of the high points of Jewish festival liturgy. The congregation rises for the *Hallel* and usually joins in the chanting of Psalms along with the cantor or prayer leader. There are dozens of melodies for the various psalms, all of them upbeat, but there is one melody in particular that I have heard sung in synagogues all over the world and that I have loved since childhood. It is a Hassidic rendering of the seven final verses of Psalm 115, and it is sung not only during *Hallel* but whenever a joyful melody is needed to add spirit to a mitzvah celebration. It is certainly familiar to all regular synagogue attenders, and it may be found in most anthologies of synagogue music (e.g., Cooperstein's *The Songs We Sing*, p. 368).

It was during my late teen years, when I was becoming increasingly impatient with the certainties and punctilios of Orthodoxy, that I was attracted to one particular verse of Psalm 115. I wondered, Did God really require that we recite the morning *Shema* before 10:00 a.m.? Did God really sentence all people to a specified period in Gehenna and only then raise them up to paradise? Did God really decree the murder of all Amalekite women and children? Did God really prescribe all of those bloody sacrifices that were not only offered in ancient times but that would be required again with the rebuilding of the temple as soon as the Messiah arrived? Did God really decree that only males could participate as leaders of public worship? And so on and on. How could the rabbis, ancient and modern, be so certain of the will of God? That we should behave with kindness and integrity toward our neighbors—*that* I could accept as the will of God. But that God still yearned for the Sabbath offering of "two he-lambs of the first year without blemish" (as specified in the Orthodox Sabbath *Mussaf* service), that I certainly could not accept.

How do human beings have the chutzpah to claim knowledge of the will of God? And so the mantra of my increasing distance from Orthodoxy became one of the verses from the *Hallel* that I sang so joyfully along with the congregation of my childhood: *The heavens belong to Adonai, and the earth was given to humanity.* I came to understand that verse to mean that we human beings have more than enough to keep us busy here on earth. How to live decently in human society should be our primary concern, and it is idle to speculate about the realms beyond. We joke about the medieval scholastics who argued about the number of angels who could fit on the head of a pin, but what about those Jewish pietists today who are certain that God will not protect a home that does not have a mezuzah and further, that God will not protect a home that *does* have a mezuzah if some of its letters are defective?

With all the welter of detail about God that can be found in the Bible, its fundamental message concerns the actions of human beings here on earth.

There is an interesting passage in the Midrash (*Sifra* 89b and elsewhere) in which two of the great second-century rabbis disagree about the greatest principle in the Torah. Rabbi Akiba chose the obvious: "*Love your neighbor as yourself*"; but Ben Azzai insisted, curiously, on Genesis 5:1: "*This is the book of the generations of man.*" Why did Ben Azzai think that this rather prosaic introductory clause was more important than the so-called Golden Rule? Because he saw it as a declaration of the equality of all human beings, all descended, as that passage continues, from a common ancestor, Adam. Every human being is, therefore, related to and responsible for every other human being.

There are two well-known passages in the Bible that attempt to answer the question, "What does Adonai ask of you?" The first, in Deuteronomy (10:12-19), after instructing us about the greatness of God and the importance of keeping God's commandments, goes on to describe God as

> *the awesome God who shows no favor and takes no bribe, but upholds*
> *the cause of the fatherless and the widow, and befriends the stranger,*
> *providing him with food and clothing. You too must befriend the*
> *stranger, for you were strangers in the land of Egypt.*

The second is that oft-repeated passage from Micah (6:6-8) that begins by asking how we may approach God. Micah rejects sacrifice as the way to God and then proceeds to answer,

> *He has told you, O man, what is good, and what Adonai requires of*
> *you—Only to do justice, and to love goodness, and to walk modestly*
> *with your God.*

What these passages have in common is the conviction that it is the actions of human beings here on earth, within the human community, that determine who is the godly person. It is not belief; it is not prayer; it is certainly not sacrifice; it is not speculation about the celestial realms, if such there be. No, "*The heavens belong to Adonai, and the earth was given to humanity.*" The overwhelming weight of Jewish tradition discourages speculation about the nature of God. Elsewhere in this volume we have written about that amazing passage in Exodus in which God informs Moses that there is no divine form but that the way we perceive of God is through God's acts: "*I will make all My goodness pass before you*" (33:19). If we are to be holy as God is holy, the way that we accomplish that is through acts of beneficence that lead us ultimately to the love of neighbor (see Lev. 19:1-18).

I cannot imagine that any other religious tradition has anywhere in its sacred literature the degree of antitheology that is evident in a passage that we find in at least three early rabbinic texts. I will quote it from the midrashic collection, *Lamentations Rabbah 2*, but it can also be found in the Jerusalem Talmud and *Pesikta d'Rav Kahana*. The third- or fourth-century sage, Rabbi Hiyya bar Abba, quotes God as explaining the calamity that befell Israel with these amazing words: "*If only they had forsaken Me but kept My law!*" Imagine! Rabbi Hiyya, and the tradition that preserved his words, suggested that it might be better to forsake God as long as we do not forsake God's law, the mitzvot that teach us how we should behave toward God's children.

What good does it do to praise and bless God, to offer sacrifices and prayers, to erect cathedrals and perform elaborate mystical rituals, if we are oblivious to the demands for justice and mercy that are the essence of God's requirements for humanity? No one said it better than Isaiah:

> *What need have I of all your sacrifices? . . .*
> *Your new moons and festivals fill Me with loathing . . .*
> *Though you pray at length, I will not listen.*
> *Your hands are stained with crime.*
> *Wash yourselves clean; put your evil doings away from My sight.*
> *Cease to do evil; learn to do good.*
> *Devote yourselves to justice; aid the wronged;*
> *Uphold the rights of the orphan; defend the cause of the widow.* (1:11-17)

Every attempt to define God makes it less likely that intelligent, well-motivated, seeking people will accept that definition. As a rabbi, I have heard it hundreds of times: How can I believe in a god who allows the innocent to suffer? How can I believe in a god who allows millions to starve? How can I believe in a god who allows bad things to happen to good people? And so on and on. Why these ceaseless questions about the justice of God? Because religionists since time immemorial have taught us that "His eye is on the sparrow," that God monitors the actions of every creature on earth and metes out punishment or reward as deserved. There is very little difference between this kind of anthropocentric, or egocentric, theology and the common medieval belief that our habitat, earth, is the center of the universe.

I will never forget the words directed to me at my Bar Mitzvah by an Orthodox rabbi. After telling me how well I had performed and all the other required platitudes, he informed me that while I should follow the mitzvot as a good Jew, I should understand that God would be watching me every moment of my life and that if I broke any of the mitzvot, I would be punished. I can still hear his final words, with his hands on my shoulders: "*Gedenk* (Remember), Shimon, God is watching you!" There were several other messages delivered at my Bar Mitzvah service, but that one, unfortunately, is the one that is emblazoned on my memory.

Why is it so difficult to believe in a god who created our universe with certain immutable laws and that it is our right to try, with all due modesty, to understand those laws, to try, as Albert Einstein put it, "to draw God's lines after him." If there is such a thing as sin, surely the worst sin is to claim the authority to speak in the name of God. Why can people not accept the idea that it is the earth, and not the heavens, which is our realm, that God gave the earth to us and what God requires of us is to act justly toward our neighbors on earth? That is what the psalmist taught us, that "*the heavens belong to God, and the earth was given to humanity.*"

People and institutions who are certain that they know the will of God, that they are acting as God's surrogates on earth, inevitably cause misery for those who might question their right to define God and to impose their definitions of the sacred on society. A few notable examples::

- The holy office of the Inquisition, which sought out heretics for the Catholic Church, believed that it was acting for the sake of heaven when it tortured and kidnapped and murdered tens of thousands of innocents in Spain, Italy, Portugal, Mexico, and elsewhere for hundreds of years.

- Islamic nations from North Africa to Indonesia are beset by mullahs and ayatollahs who stir up murderous jihadists for the sake of heaven as they insist they understand it. And so Shiite kills Sunni and Sunni kills Shiite, and both kill anyone who might question the truth and the hegemony of Islam.

- Fundamentalist Christian preachers dispute the findings of sociology and science—be it in regard to stem cells, the origins of life, or the rights of women—for the sake of heaven. Some forbid certain essential medical services; some go from door to door seeking to share "God's truth" with the benighted; some promise God's healing to those who lay their hands on their television sets. They, and only they, know the mind of God and they are more than willing to impose their sure knowledge on everyone else.

- In the otherwise democratic state of Israel, the rigid Orthodox minority wields inordinate power over the state. Acting "for the sake of heaven," they impose medieval standards on an increasingly restive population, alienating them from their religious heritage. It is this kind of certainty that leads to the extremism of a Baruch Goldstein, the murderer of Hebron; or a Yigal Amir, the murderer of Yitzhak Rabin; and to a group of rabbis who decreed that people were killed in terrorist attacks because the mezuzot on their doorposts were flawed.

- Several years ago, in my capacity as president of our local board of rabbis, I had the occasion to meet privately with the cardinal of our archdiocese. Somehow our conversation turned to the multiplicity of denominations within the broader family of American Christendom. I had to stifle my amazement when this distinguished Prince of the Church delivered himself of the following observation: "I cannot understand why all these other churches have to find complicated and contradictory routes to God. We Roman Catholics have a clear and unobstructed pathway to heaven; why can't they accept it?" Politeness prevented me from reminding him that his "unobstructed pathway to heaven" included the consignment of thousands of my ancestors to the flames of the auto da fe.

If only they could forget about heaven! When Rabbi Hiyya delivered his remarkable dictum, he was not suggesting that one should cease to believe in God. The passage in *Lamentations Rabba* goes on to suggest that by keeping the laws of the Torah, "the light which it contains will lead them back to the right path." One would hope that a person who chooses to act in accordance with the laws of beneficence that are found in the Torah and the prophets would come to believe in God. But it is not the belief that is essential in Judaism; it is the act.

I must confess that I do often speculate about the qualities of God, but I know that there are mysteries beyond the comprehension of the human mind, mysteries about which only "heaven knows." For many years, I have thought of God as a dependable friend, as an undefinable presence with whom I can share my innermost thoughts, my joys, and my sorrows. All too often, as I observe the acts of individuals, religious groups, and governments, I imagine myself sitting on a mourning stool commiserating with God. But I do not ask God to answer my "why," because I know that God might ask me the very same question.

Are there problems here on earth? Certainly, more than any human being might hope to solve within a lifetime. But that is our task and our sacred mission. I am more than content to leave heavenly problems to God as I believe that God has assigned the earthly problems—hunger, war, hatred, greed, exploitation, etc., to us. And so the next time that I celebrate a festival, I will sing out, with as much gusto as I can, "*Ha-shamayim shamayim l'Adonai ve'ha-aretz natan liv'nei adam* (The heavens belong to God, and the earth was given to humanity)."

Turn 24

*I had a dream,
and my spirit is troubled.*

—Daniel 2:3

We'll begin this final "turn" with a little quiz. What do the following biblical characters have in common: Jacob, Nebuchadnezzar, a Midianite soldier, King Solomon, and Daniel? No answer? All right, a hint. Add to that list the hungry man and the thirsty man in a parable by Isaiah and also the false prophets condemned by Moses and later by Jeremiah. Ah, some of you are smiling, but most of you are still puzzled. So, my final hint. Add to that list Joseph, Pharaoh, and the Pharaoh's butler and baker. Ah, now you've got it. They were all dreamers. If you want to check the references before you ask "So what?" here they are,

- Jacob's dream vision at Beth El, Genesis 28:12

- Nebuchadnezzar's portentous dream interpreted by Daniel, Daniel 2:1

- The Midianite soldier who dreamed of the destructive barley bread, Judges 7:13

- King Solomon's dream request for wisdom; 1 Kings 3:5

- Daniel, Belshazzar's dream interpreter, himself has a dream, Daniel 7:1

- Isaiah's evocation of hungry and thirsty dreamers, Isaiah 29:8

- Moses' and Jeremiah's condemnations of the dreams of false prophets, Deuteronomy 13:2 and Jeremiah 23:25

- Joseph, the quintessential dreamer and dream interpreter, Genesis 37:5, *et seq.*

- Pharaoh's double dream that resulted in the elevation of Joseph, Genesis 41:1

- Pharaoh's butler and baker who told their dreams to Joseph, Genesis 40:5.

There are many other instances in the Bible of visions, notably Ezekiel's vision of the valley of dry bones (chap. 37); Isaiah's temple vision (chap. 6); and Samuel's first encounter with God (1 Sam. 3) which may or may not have been dreams, but all of the instances cited above are clearly labeled as dreams. And now you may ask, So what?

I don't think that I am unique in revealing that I have been fascinated by the question of where dreams come from since childhood. From my earliest Torah teachers, I learned that God inspired the dreams of Jacob and Joseph, of Pharaoh's butler and baker, and of Pharaoh himself. When I was about the age of the young Samuel, I wondered if God would some night awaken me with the call "Shimon! Shimon!" so that I, too, might answer, "*Hineni* (Here I am)." And it was at about that time that I first became aware of a prayer that was recited in my childhood synagogue on all of the major festivals when the *kohanim* (descendants, real or supposed, of Aaron) ascended the bimah to chant *Birkat Kohanim*, the priestly benediction, which, according to tradition, was first revealed to Moses and Aaron (Num. 6:22 *ff*).

For those who are not familiar with the ritual of *Birkat Kohanim*, which is never practiced in Reform or Reconstructionist synagogues, rarely if ever in Conservative synagogues, and omitted today even by some Orthodox congregations, it might be well to describe it. Men, and only men, who believe that they are *kohanim*, fulfill three functions in the Orthodox community: (1) they receive the honor of the first *aliyah* whenever the Torah is read; (2) they "redeem" firstborn sons in the ceremony called *Pidyon Ha-Ben*; and (3) they bless the congregation—in most Orthodox synagogues only on the festivals but in some, especially in Israel, on many other occasions—during the cantor's repetition of the *Amidah* prayer. The ritual begins with the removal of their shoes, the washing of their hands by Levites, their ascent to the bimah, and the enwrapping of their entire bodies, head included, in the *tallit*.

So sacred is this ritual (usually called *duchenen*) that the congregation is not supposed to look directly at the *kohanim* from the moment when they recite the opening *b'racha* of the ritual until they have completed the benediction. While still in knee pants, I was warned that I might go blind if I looked at the *kohanim* during *duchenen*. (A few years later, I was warned that I might go blind if I did other forbidden things.) Rather than looking toward the pulpit during these sacred moments, congregants are supposed to look into their prayer books and read a very unusual prayer in an undertone after each of the first two verses of the benediction. It is this prayer, recited only during the *duchenen*, that I was introduced to, as I said above, as an impressionable child who was curious about the origin of dreams.

This prayer, with some minor additions, is taken directly from the Talmud (*Berakhot* 55b) and is prescribed there to be recited before a kohen by a person who has had a dream which he does not understand. I reproduce it here in its entirety:

> *Sovereign of the universe: I am Yours and my dreams are Yours. I have dreamt a dream, and I do not know what it means. May it be Your will, Adonai my God and God of my fathers, that all my dreams, for me and for all Israel, should result in good, whether I have dreamt about myself or whether I have dreamt about others or whether others have dreamt about me. If they are good [dreams], strengthen and reinforce them and confirm them for me or for others, like the dreams of Joseph the righteous. And if they require healing, heal them like Hezekiah, king of Judah, from his illness, and like Miriam, the prophetess, from her leprosy, and like Naaman from his leprosy, and like the waters of bitterness by the hands of Moses our teacher, and like the waters of Jericho by the hands of Elisha. And as you transformed the curse of the wicked Balaam from a curse into a blessing, thus may You transform all of my dreams, for me and for all Israel, to good, and may You watch over me and be merciful to me and accept me.*

So intrigued was I by that prayer that I could recite it by heart well before my Bar Mitzvah. Carefully looking away from the bimah, I would read the first half of it after the first verse of the benediction and the second half after the second verse. One side benefit of this regimen was that I had to find out who Hezekiah and Naaman and Elisha were; I was already familiar with the Pentateuchal references. My father, of course, rather than simply telling me their stories, answered my queries by sitting me down with a Bible and directing me to the appropriate chapters in the book of 2 Kings. And when

I asked him if it was really true that all our dreams come from God, he answered, albeit with some hesitation, yes, hoping that I would be satisfied. And I was . . . for a while.

What child could be anything but fascinated by the story of Pharaoh's dreams? One is tempted to say that it comes straight out of the *Arabian Nights*, except that it preceded those seductive stories by several centuries. There is the all-powerful king, his magicians and wise men, the young Israelite slave boy, the interpretation offered humbly in the name of God, and the rise from rags to riches. But then, later in life, I came across another dream story and could not help but notice the parallels. This second dream is in the book of Daniel, and there we find the all-powerful king of Babylonia, Nebuchadnezzar, his "magicians and enchanters and sorcerers and Chaldeans," the young Israelite exile, the interpretation offered humbly in the name of "*God in heaven who reveals mysteries*," and then the honors heaped on the young Daniel. (The Belshazzar dream comes later in the book.)

Both episodes begin with the monarch demanding the interpretation of a dream that he realizes has an important message. It was actually Nebuchadnezzar who said, "*I had a dream, and my spirit is troubled to know the dream*," but Pharaoh expressed the same request to his courtiers. And both episodes conclude with the promotion of the young Israelite (more properly, the Judean in the case of Daniel) interpreter to high estate. Let's compare the rewards:

> *So Pharaoh said to Joseph: "Since God has made all this known to you, there is none so discerning and wise as you. You shall be in charge of my court, and by your command shall all my people be directed; only with respect to the throne shall I be superior to you." Pharaoh further said to Joseph: "See, I put you in charge of all the land of Egypt."*
> (Gen. 41:39-41)

> *Then King Nebuchadnezzar . . . said to Daniel: "Truly your God is the God of Gods and Lord of Kings, and a revealer of mysteries, for you have been able to reveal this mystery," Then the king gave Daniel high honors and many great gifts, and made him ruler over the whole province of Babylon, and chief prefect over all the wise men of Babylon.*
> (Dan. 2:46-48)

I must make mention of one additional parallel in these two stories before going on with our inquiry into the source of dreams. In the Genesis story, the Israelite Joseph does what no other man can do in interpreting the dream of the Egyptian monarch. In the Daniel story, the Judean Daniel does what no other man can do in interpreting the dream of the Babylonian monarch. While I feel certain that the author who first transcribed the story of Joseph believed that this story, received from previous generations, was literally true—that is, that God had set all the complex events in motion so that Joseph could emerge as viceroy and bring his tribe down to Egypt—such is not the case with the author of the Daniel story.

The book of Daniel, like the Christian book of Revelation, is an apocalyptic work. It is the invention of an author who, in time of great upheaval and uncertainty, used symbolic language and familiar names to predict a far better future, a time of triumph and peace. The author found the name Daniel in the book of Ezekiel where he is cited as an example of wisdom and piety and of course, he found the Joseph story in Genesis. It is quite likely that the author was a Judean who lived under the persecution of the Seleucids in the second pre-Christian century and he used the downfall of the powerful Babylonian kings, Nebuchadnezzar and Belshazzar, to predict the desired downfall of the cruel Hellenist king, Antiochus.

What is interesting for our purposes is the fact that this Jew, who lived just before the dawn of the rabbinic era, was convinced of the importance of dreams. The main substance of the book consists of two dreams by Nebuchadnezzar, Daniel's dream, and then a series of dreamlike visions by Daniel, all of which employ symbols to foretell future events. This fascination with dreams is something that I recognize in myself and that I believe has permeated Jewish tradition from the days of Joseph down to the days of Sigmund Freud and beyond.

There are literally scores of dreams described in classical rabbinic literature and even more opinions about the importance or lack of importance of dreams. There are comments on the symbolism in dreams, the interpretation of dreams, puns in dreams, the power of dreams, and dreams as prophecy. The richest source of material on dreams may be found in the Talmudic tractate *Berachot*, folios 55b through 57b; and there we find a statement by Rabbi Jonathan (third-century Palestine) that might as easily have come from the pen of Sigmund Freud: "*A man is shown in a dream only what is suggested by his own thoughts.*" But other eminent sages suggested that there was an element of the supernatural in dreams. Rabbi Hanina ben Isaac opined that "*dreams are an incomplete form of prophecy*" (*Genesis Rabba* 17:5) while a certain Rabbi Joseph took dreams so seriously that he decreed that "*if one is placed under the ban of excommunication in a dream, ten men are required to annul the ban*" (*Nedarim* 8a).

The *Berachot* material refers to twenty-four professional dream interpreters in Jerusalem alone, which certainly attests to the importance that the people ascribed to dreams. Like Joseph's Pharaoh and Daniel's Nebuchadnezzar, the people felt the need for reassurance after experiencing enigmatic dreams. They wanted interpretations of shalom (Gen. 41:16) as Joseph promised to Pharaoh. Most of the rabbis tended to dismiss these Jerusalem professionals as charlatans, and the great second-century sage, Rabbi Meir, brushed the speculation aside with the comment that "*dreams do not help and do not harm*" (*Gittin* 52a). But a century later, the Babylonian sage Rav warned that it would be wise to fast after a bad dream (*Shabbat* 11b).

Having referred above to Freud, there is a passage in the *Berachot* material (56b) which, if it were written seventeen centuries later, might be read as a parody of Freudian dream analysis. And for anyone who thinks of the Talmud as a collection of dry legalistic casuistry, this passage should serve as a corrective:

> *A certain sectarian said to Rabbi Ishmael: I saw myself [in a dream] pouring oil on olives. He replied: [This man] had intercourse with his mother. He said to him: I dreamt I plucked a star. He replied: You have stolen an Israelite. He said to him: I dreamt I swallowed the star. He replied: You have sold an Israelite and consumed the proceeds. He said to him: I dreamt that my eyes were kissing each other. He replied: [This man] had intercourse with his sister. He said to him: I dreamt that I kissed the moon. He replied: He had intercourse with the wife of an Israelite. I dreamt I was walking in the shade of a myrtle. He replied: He has outraged a betrothed damsel. He said to him: I dreamed that there was a shade above me, and yet it was beneath me. He replied: It means unnatural intercourse. He said to him: I saw ravens keep on coming to my bed. He replied: Your wife has misconducted herself with many men. He said to him: I saw pigeons keep coming to my bed. He replied: You have defiled many women . . .*

Freud, who taught us that certain thoughts which are suppressed while we are conscious reappear from the subconscious in dreams, would seem to have been a worthy descendant of Joseph and Daniel. No, I do not believe that dreams are messages from God. But I do believe that they are promptings from the subconscious and that, as such, they should be mulled over in an attempt to discover what it is that might be bothering us, what it is that we should understand about ourselves. Come to think of it, maybe that is a message from God.

*　　*　　*

There is a rabbinic tradition that teaches that one should conclude the study of text on an upbeat, with a verse of encouragement. Having concluded this volume with an essay on dreams, I have chosen this verse from the prophecy of Joel as my final word (until the next collection of "turns"):

> *You shall know that I am in the midst of Israel*
> *and that I, Adonai, am your God, and there is none else.*
> *And My people shall never again be put to shame.*
> *And it will come to pass that I will pour out my spirit on all flesh;*
> *your sons and your daughters shall prophesy,*
> *your old men shall dream dreams,*
> *and your young men shall see visions. (Joel 2:27-3:1)*

Acknowledgments

There are many people—teachers, friends, family—who have exemplified Torah for me and to whom I am eternally grateful. I take this opportunity to acknowledge them, especially those who in the past few years encouraged me in the writing of this book. But I must begin with *Avi Mori*, my father-teacher, of blessed memory, whose teachings long preceded any notion of this book. My father made it clear to me at a very early age that he wanted me to be worthy of the generations of rabbis from whom we are descended. Back then I resented and often attempted to thwart his expectations, but year by year I came to realize how much I had learned from him, if only through the osmosis of proximity. He was a font of wit and wisdom, deeply rooted in Torah. I hope that these essays demonstrate that I took seriously the admonition of Proverbs 3:1 and that I inherited from him considerably more than his love for the Red Sox and fishing.

I am the facilitator for a group of thoughtful and congenial Mainiacs who, for the past six years, have joined me each Shabbat morning from June through October on the campus of Bowdoin College to study Torah. The insights that spring from their lips are truly remarkable. At one of our sessions, after I had said about a particular verse that I loved it, my wife (to whom this book is dedicated) remarked: "You say that about every verse!" And I realized that she was right, as in so many other things. If not literally "every" biblical verse, I do love hundreds of them. And so I began to think: Could I possibly convey to a wider audience my love for some of these favorite verses, how I take pleasure in turning them over and over again as they reveal ever more lovely variations. And so this book, inspired in no small measure by the members of the Bowdoin Torah Havurah. My thanks to them and to the president of Bowdoin College, Barry Mills, and the Head Librarian, Sherrie Bergman, who welcome us to the campus each year.

My thanks also to Aron Hirt-Manheimer, Editor, and Joy Weinberg, Managing Editor, of the excellent magazine, *Reform Judaism,* published quarterly by the Union for Reform Judaism. They have graciously edited and published a number of my essays over the years, including, in abridged form, a few that appear in this volume.

Special thanks to rabbi, author and notable *mensch,* Harold Kushner, for his encouragement and advice in the earliest stages of this book, and to Eric Yoffie, president of the Union for Reform Judaism, who has devoted his presidency to the literacy and the liberality of North American Jewry. In my Foreword to this volume, I make mention of my childhood teacher, Abe Ruderman, who, although I did not realize it at the time, introduced me to the process of *midrash*. He produced one of America's leading Jewish scholars, David Ruderman, director of the Center for Advanced Jewish Studies at the University of Pennsylvania. I thank him also for his encouragement and his friendship.

I was delighted when Civia Rosenberg, an old friend and member of the Bowdoin Havurah, volunteered herself and her daughter Ilana Rosenberg of Ilanadesign to do the inspired art work for this book. They realized immediately what it was that I wanted to convey. I am grateful to both of them.

And finally, thanks to the members of my four congregations, the Monroe Temple of Liberal Judaism (Monroe, NY), United Portuguese Israelite Congregation Mikve Israel—Emanuel (Curacao, Neth. Antilles), K.A.M. Isaiah Israel (Chicago) and Cong. Keneseth Israel (Elkins Park, PA) for their patience and, in most cases, their willingness to question and to learn. I thank them all, in the spirit of Ben Zoma who taught (*Avot* 4:1): *Who is wise? The person who learns from every one, as it is written (Psalms 119: 99):* "*From all of my teachers I have derived understanding.*"

About the Author

Simeon J. Maslin was born and raised in Winthrop, Massachusetts, the son of the cantor of the town's Orthodox synagogue. He received his early education in the Winthrop schools, Yeshiva University High School, and Hebrew Teachers' College. After receiving his BA from Harvard, he went on to graduate studies in governmental administration at the Wharton School, receiving his MA from the University of Pennsylvania. It was while working with the Hillel directors at Harvard and Penn that Maslin began considering a career in the rabbinate. He decided to go on to Hebrew Union College in Cincinnati after being encouraged by faculty members at the Brandeis Camp Institute.

After his ordination in 1954, Rabbi Maslin went on to pulpits in Monroe, New York, Curacao, Netherlands Antilles, Chicago, and Philadelphia. After forty-three years in the pulpit rabbinate, including stints as the president of the Chicago Board of Rabbis, the Philadelphia Board of Rabbis, and the Central Conference of American Rabbis, he retired and has since been writing, lecturing, traveling, and enjoying the coast of Maine. His five-year tenure as rabbi of the historic congregation in Curacao (1651) encouraged him to volunteer his services to overseas congregations after retirement, including Cape Town and other cities in South Africa, Perth, Australia, and Singapore.

Rabbi Maslin is the recipient of a doctor of ministry degree from Chicago Theological Seminary (United Church of Christ) and an honorary DD from Hebrew Union College-Jewish Institute of Religion. He is the author of numerous articles and two previous books. He is married to Judith Blumberg Maslin, and they are the parents of three children and the grandparents of ten—their own beloved minyan.

Index

Biblical Citations

Talmudic and Midrashic Citations

General Index